How to Say No and Gain Respect

A Biblical Guide to Setting Boundaries and Living with Purpose

Rodney A. Lindemann

Rev. Rodney A. Lindemann

ISBN: 979-8-9932274-2-9 (Hardbound)
ISBN: 979-8-9932274-0-5 (Paperback)
ISBN: 979-8-9932274-1-2 (eBook)

Rodney A. Lindemann
www.PastorRodLindemann.com
For information about special discounts for bulk purchases or speaking engagements contact Pastor Rod Lindemann through the website.

Web: www.PastorRodLindemann
Facebook: www.https://www.facebook.com/PastorRodLindemann
Instagram: https://www.instagram.com/pastorrodlindemann

Contents

Dedication

To my cherished wife, Miriam, my Proverbs 31,

You have been my faithful partner through seasons of overwhelming "yeses"
and the difficult journey of learning to say "no."
Your wisdom and grace have helped me find my best "yes"—for God,
for our family, and for the life we are building together.
All my love, always. -Rod

Prologue

The Yes That Cost Me Everything

For most of my life, and especially in my years as a pastor, "yes" was the easiest and most automatic word in my vocabulary. It felt like the right answer, the spiritual answer. A request from a congregant? Yes. An invitation to join another committee? Yes. An opportunity to serve, even when my own tank was empty? Yes, of course. I wore my endless affirmations like a badge of honor, believing I was living out the ultimate servant's calling.

The truth is, I had become a victim of my own inability to say no. Each "yes" was a step on a path that led not to fulfillment, but to a deep, soul-crushing burnout. The mental fatigue became a constant fog, and the joy I once found in ministry was slowly being choked out by the sheer weight of my commitments.

The title of this book, How to Say No and Gain Respect, isn't a clever marketing phrase I came up with recently. It's a lifeline that first came to my mind over fifteen years ago, during the very season I was realizing the "yeses" in my life were no longer obtainable. I had hit a wall. My well was dry. I had nothing left to give anyone—not my church, not my family, and certainly not myself.

This isn't just a pastor's story. In my years of ministry, I've seen this same exhaustion in the eyes of the most dedicated lay people serving in the church. The Sunday school teachers, the small group leaders, the volunteers who show up for everything—they too often serve until they have nothing left, fearing that a "no" would be a sign of a weak faith or a selfish heart.

This book was written from the lessons learned in the trenches of that experience—a journey through burnout that ultimately led to my early retirement. It's the guide I wish I'd had. It's the permission slip I needed to set boundaries, not as a way to push people away, but as a way to preserve a joyful and freely given "yes" for where God was truly calling me to serve. It is my prayer that my story can help you reclaim your own.

Maybe you're asking these question: "Lord, is this what you wanted? A servant who is faithful to everyone but his own family? A worker who is so busy for you that he has no time to be with you?"

It's time to follow a new path – a new journey!

Rod Lindemann

Introduction

The Freedom of a Godly "No"

Does your life feel like your own?

Or does it feel like a series of obligations, a calendar overflowing with the priorities of others, and a constant, low-grade anxiety that you are letting everyone down? You are a good person. You are a person of faith. You want to love your neighbor, serve your church, excel in your career, and be there for your family. You have a servant's heart. And so, you say "yes."

You say "yes" to the extra project at work, even though it means another late night. You say "yes" to the new ministry role, even though you already feel stretched thin. You say "yes" to the friend in need, even though you are emotionally and physically exhausted. You say "yes" because it feels like the right thing to do, the Christian thing to do. To say "no," you fear, would be selfish, unloving, or a sign of a weak faith.

And yet, in the quiet moments, a different feeling surfaces. It is the bitter taste of resentment. It is the heavy weight of burnout. It is the profound loneliness of feeling that no one sees the real you—the you who is tired, who has limits, who has dreams and callings of your own that are being perpetually pushed to the side. You live under the tyranny of "yes," and you are beginning to suspect that this life of frantic, joyless service is not the abundant life that Jesus promised.

If this resonates with you, you are not alone. And you are not wrong.

This book is built on a simple but life-altering premise: the undisciplined, boundary-less life is not the high calling of a Christian; it is a misunderstanding of what it means to love. The path to a life of deeper freedom, greater purpose, and more authentic relationships is not found in saying "yes" more, but in learning the courageous and holy art of saying "no."

We are going to embark on a journey to reclaim this lost art. We will discover that the concept of boundaries is not a modern psychological invention, but a divine principle woven into the fabric of creation and modeled perfectly in the life of Christ. We will journey inward to confront the two great enemies of a bounded life—the fear of man and the weight of false guilt—and learn to replace them with a reverential awe of God and a clear conscience. We will then look outward, equipping you with the practical, grace-filled language to speak the truth in love, to stand firm when your limits are tested, and to build the kind of relationships that are based not on obligation, but on mutual honor and respect.

The goal is not to become a person who rejects others, but to become the person God created you to be—a wise steward of your one precious life. The purpose of a strategic "no" is to create the space for a more wholehearted, joyful, and effective "yes" to the things that truly matter. This is the path from being a people-pleaser to being a God-pleaser. It is the journey to trading the shallow approval of others for the deep, lasting respect that comes from a life of integrity. It is the courageous step into the freedom you were saved for.

Let's begin our journey...

In his heart a man determines his course,
but the Lord determines his steps.

Proverbs 16:9

Chapter One

In the Beginning: Boundaries

Before we can learn how to say no, we must first understand why we can. For many of us, the very concept of setting boundaries feels deeply uncomfortable, perhaps even unchristian. It can feel selfish, restrictive, or unkind. We picture walls being built, people being pushed away, and needs being unmet. The modern conversation around boundaries is often framed in the language of pop psychology and self-help, which can make a person of faith wary. Is this just the world's way of baptizing selfishness and calling it self-care? Is the act of saying "no" simply a resignation of our call to love, serve, and bear one another's burdens?

These are valid questions that deserve a serious, biblically-grounded answer. And the answer is found not in the latest bestseller list, but in the very first lines of Scripture. The truth is that boundaries are not a human invention; they are a divine principle. They are not a concession to our fallen world, but a feature of God's perfect creation. Before there was sin, before there was humanity, before there was even a world as we know it, there were boundaries. Our God is a God of beautiful, life-giving, and holy limits. To understand the power and godliness of a well-placed "no," we must go back to the beginning, to see how God Himself, in His infinite wisdom and love, first created a world of glorious order out of a formless void. It was an act of creation that began not with a "yes," but with a profound and powerful act of separation.

The Cosmic "No": God the Boundary-Setter

The opening of Genesis is one of the most majestic passages in all of literature. It is poetic, powerful, and foundational to our entire worldview. But have you ever read it through the lens of boundary-setting? When we do, we discover that the creation of the universe was a masterclass in establishing limits. The text tells us that in the beginning, "the earth was formless and void, and darkness was over the surface of the deep" (Genesis 1:2). This is a picture of chaos. It is a world without definition, without structure, without limits. It is a canvas without lines, a song without rhythm, a story without grammar. And God's first act is to speak into this chaos and begin the sacred work of separation.

On the first day, God says, "Let there be light," and there was light. But He doesn't stop there. The very next thing He does is create a distinction. "God separated the light from the darkness. God called the light day, and the darkness He called night" (Genesis 1:4-5). This is the first boundary. It is a fundamental division that orders our entire existence. This is not merely a physical separation; it is a profound theological statement. Throughout Scripture, light represents God's presence, truth, goodness, and order, while darkness represents chaos, ignorance, and sin. God's very first creative act was to draw a line, to say, in effect, "This is not that." He established that there is a difference, and in that difference, there is goodness and order. He created a rhythm for life—a time for work and a time for rest, a time for light and a time for dark. This boundary was not restrictive; it was creative. It gave the world its first taste of structure.

The work continues on the second day. God creates an "expanse" to separate "the waters which were below the expanse from the waters which were above the expanse" (Genesis 1:7). He is creating defined spaces. He is pushing back the chaos of the watery deep to make a safe, habitable pocket for life to flourish. He is establishing the heavens and the sky, giving the world its vertical dimension. He is building the architecture of the universe, and He is doing it by setting limits, by separating one thing from another. This act of creating an atmosphere, a breathable and protected space, is an act of loving boundary-setting. He is defining what is safe and what is not, what is for humanity and what is for the heavens.

This theme reaches its climax on the third day when God speaks the most tangible boundary yet into existence. "Let the waters below the heavens be gathered into one place, and let the dry land appear" (Genesis 1:9). Here, God sets a limit on the most powerful and chaotic force in the ancient imagination: the sea. For ancient peoples, the sea was a symbol of chaos, terror, and untamable power. Yet God, with a simple command, puts it in its place. He draws a line in the sand and tells the ocean, "You may come this far, but no farther."

The prophet Jeremiah reflects on this awesome power centuries later, speaking for God: "Do you not fear Me?' declares the LORD. 'Do you not tremble in My presence? For I have placed the sand as a boundary for the sea, an everlasting barrier which it cannot cross. Though the waves toss, they cannot prevail; though they roar, they cannot cross it'" (Jeremiah 5:22).

Think about the profound truth here. The very existence of the land we stand on is thanks to a divine boundary. Without this limit, life as we know it would be impossible. God's boundary on the sea was not an act of limitation in a negative sense; it was an act of creation in the most positive sense. It created the very possibility for trees to grow, for animals to roam, and for humans to build homes.

What does this tell us about the character of our God? It tells us that He is a God of order, not of chaos. He values distinction, definition, and purpose. His creative power is expressed through His ability to set wise and life-giving limits. Our own innate desire for order, for a schedule that works, for a home that is not cluttered, for relationships that are clearly defined—this is not a mere personality quirk. It is a reflection of the image of our Creator, the one who first brought order to the cosmos by setting things in their proper place. Just as a composer uses measures and rests—boundaries of time and sound—to create beautiful music out of noise, so God uses boundaries to create a beautiful and flourishing world out of a formless void. Without limits, there is no art. Without boundaries, there is no creation.

The Personal "No": A Loving Boundary in the Garden

After establishing the grand, cosmic boundaries that shape our universe, God zooms in. He plants a garden and, in an act of breathtaking intimacy, forms the first man from the dust of the ground He just created. Here, the divine principle of boundary-setting moves from the cosmic to the personal, from the planetary to the relational. And it is here that we see the true heart behind God's holy limits.

It is crucial that we see the context in which God establishes His first boundary with humanity. It is a context of overwhelming abundance and freedom. God's first word to Adam is not one of restriction, but of extravagant permission. "The LORD God commanded the man, saying, 'From any tree of the garden you may eat freely'" (Genesis 2:16). Let that sink in. Any tree. Eat freely. This is not the language of a restrictive tyrant looking to control his subjects. This is the language of a generous and loving Father delighting in providing for His child. The Garden is a world of "yes." Yes to the fruit, yes to the beauty, yes to the fellowship with God, yes to the meaningful work of cultivating the land.

It is only within this vast landscape of "yes" that God places one, single, solitary "no." He continues, "...but from the tree of the knowledge of good and evil you shall not eat, for in the day that you eat from it you will surely die" (Genesis 2:17).

For centuries, people have misunderstood this command. It has been painted as an arbitrary test, a divine tripwire designed to make Adam and Eve fail. But when we see it through the lens of God's character as a boundary-setter, we understand it in a completely different light. This boundary was not a test of obedience for the sake of it; it was an act of loving protection.

First and foremost, the boundary was for their protection. God was protecting them from a reality they were not created to bear: the experiential knowledge of evil. They knew only good. They lived in a state of perfect innocence, with no shame, no fear, no guilt. The knowledge of evil would introduce these poisons into their souls, and as God warned, it would lead to death—spiritual, relational, and eventually, physical.

Think of a loving parent who tells their toddler, "You can play with any toy in this room, but you must not touch the hot stove." Is that command about limiting the child's fun? Is it an arbitrary test of the child's obedience? Of course not. It is a boundary born of love and superior wisdom, designed to protect the child from severe harm. The parent knows the pain of a burn, and they set a limit to spare their beloved child from that pain. In the same way, God, our Heavenly Father, knew the devastating pain of sin and death, and He set a boundary to protect His children from it.

Second, the boundary was the foundation of their relationship. Love, to be genuine, requires a choice. Without the option to say "no," a "yes" is meaningless. This single boundary gave Adam and Eve a tangible way to trust God. By choosing not to eat from the tree, they were actively saying, "We trust Your goodness, Father. We believe that Your wisdom is greater than our curiosity. We choose Your will over our own." It was the anchor of their relationship, the daily opportunity to exercise faith and love. A world with no boundaries, with no opportunity to choose obedience, would be a world of robots, not of sons and daughters in a loving relationship with their Father.

Finally, the boundary was a reminder of their identity. It was a gentle, constant reminder of reality: they were the creatures, and God was the Creator. He knew all things, and they were dependent on His wisdom. The tree represented a desire to be "like God" (Genesis 3:5), to usurp His role as the definer of good and evil. The boundary was a call to humility, to rest in their identity as beloved children, rather than striving to be gods themselves. It kept them in a right and peaceful relationship with reality.

The Broken Boundary and the In-Rush of Chaos

The tragedy of Genesis 3 is the story of a perfect, loving boundary being questioned, doubted, and ultimately, violated. The serpent's temptation is a direct assault on the goodness of God's limit. His first question is designed to sow doubt: "Indeed, has God said, 'You shall not eat from any tree of the garden'?"

(Genesis 3:1). He twists God's abundant "yes" into a restrictive "no." He then directly contradicts God's warning, promising, "You surely will not die!" (Genesis 3:4). He reframes God's protective boundary as a jealous restriction, suggesting that God is holding something good back from them.

When Adam and Eve chose to believe this lie and step across the line God had drawn in love, the consequences were immediate and catastrophic. The order of the Garden was shattered, and the chaos that God had pushed back in creation came rushing into the human experience.

The protection the boundary offered was gone. The first thing they experienced was shame, and they tried to cover themselves. The intimacy they shared with God was replaced by fear, and they hid from His presence. The harmony they had with each other was broken, replaced by blame and accusation. The peace they had with creation was shattered, replaced with a curse of thorns, thistles, and painful toil.

The story of the Fall is the ultimate testament to the goodness of God's boundaries. It shows us that when we defy the wise and loving limits our Creator has established, the result is not freedom, but bondage. The result is not enlightenment, but darkness. The result is not life, but death. The chaos that was "formless and void" at the beginning of creation now entered the human heart.

Conclusion: Reclaiming Our Divine Design

So where does this leave us, living on this side of the broken boundary? It leaves us with a profound and hopeful truth: the desire for boundaries is not selfish; it is a part of our original design. The longing you feel for order in your schedule, for peace in your home, for health in your relationships—that is the echo of Eden. It is the image of a boundary-setting God, stamped upon your soul, crying out for the restoration of order in a world of chaos.

Before you can learn the scripts for saying no, or the strategies for dealing with pushback, you must settle this foundational truth in your heart. Setting a boundary is not, at its core, an act of rejection. It is an act of creation. It is you, as a sub-creator made in the image of God, bringing order to your own little corner of the world. It is you separating the light from the darkness in your own life. It is you telling the chaotic sea of demands, "You may come this far, but no farther." It is you protecting the garden of your soul, your family, and your calling so that life can flourish there.

To deny yourself the permission to set boundaries is to deny a fundamental aspect of how God made you and how He manages the entire universe. It is to accept a life that is "formless and void" when you were created for purpose and order. As we continue this journey, we will build upon this foundation, learning the practical skills needed to implement this divine principle. But for now, let us rest in this truth. Our God is a God of good and perfect boundaries, and He invites us to be like Him.

Reflection Questions:

1. How does viewing God as the first and ultimate boundary-setter change your perception of setting limits in your own life? Does it make the idea feel more sacred and less selfish?

2. Consider the areas of your own life that feel "formless and void"—your schedule, your finances, your relationships, your digital habits. Where might a single, God-honoring boundary begin to bring much-needed order?

3. Reflect on God's boundary in the Garden. It came in a context of immense freedom and was designed for protection and relationship. How can this model shape the way you think about setting your own boundaries—not as acts of restriction, but as acts of love for yourself and others?

4. Think about a time you ignored a wise boundary, whether it was one you set for yourself or one set by someone who cared for you. What were the

consequences? How did it affect your relationship with God, yourself, or others?

A Prayer for a Bounded Life

Heavenly Father, Creator of the universe, thank you for being a God of order and not of chaos. Thank you for the wisdom and love you showed in the very beginning, separating the light from the darkness and setting a shore for the sea. Forgive me for the times I have believed the lie that boundaries are unloving. Help me to see the boundaries in my own life as you see them: as tools of creation, protection, and love. Grant me the wisdom to see where order is needed and the courage to set the limits that will honor You and allow true fruit to grow. Amen.

Chapter Two

The Law of Love: Boundaries in the Old Testament

If our understanding that boundaries begin with God's creative act in Genesis, it finds its relational blueprint in the Law given to Moses on Mount Sinai. For many, the phrase "Old Testament Law" conjures images of stone tablets, rigid rules, and a stern, finger-wagging deity. It can feel like a departure from the loving, creative Father we met in the Garden. The Law can seem like an endless list of "thou shalt nots," a heavy yoke of restriction placed upon a rebellious people. And if we view it that way, it's easy to dismiss it as a dated and irrelevant legal code, one that was thankfully superseded by the grace we find in the New Testament. But this perspective misses the profound love story at the heart of the Law.

The Law was not given to a random people to prove they could be good enough for God. It was given to a redeemed people. God did not stand at the border of Egypt and say, "If you follow these 613 rules perfectly, I will rescue you from Pharaoh." He rescued them first. He parted the Red Sea, broke the chains of their slavery, and carried them into the wilderness on eagles' wings, all by His grace. The Law, then, was given to this newly freed people not as a means of earning their salvation, but as a guide for how to live in it. It was a loving Father's instruction manual to His children, showing them how to build a flourishing, just, and holy community that would be a light to the nations. It was a framework for freedom.

Imagine rescuing a group of people who had only ever known slavery. Their entire identity was shaped by the whims of cruel taskmasters. They had no concept of self-governance, healthy relationships, or personal responsibility. How would you teach them to be free? You would give them a structure. You would provide a constitution that defines their rights and responsibilities, protecting them from the chaos of their former lives and from harming one another. This is what the Law was for Israel. It was a divine framework of relational boundaries, designed to protect their relationship with God and their relationships with each other. It was, in its very essence, a Law of Love.

Vertical Boundaries: Loving God with All Your Heart

The foundation of this new community was its relationship with its rescuer, Yahweh. Before Israel could learn to love their neighbors, they had to learn to love their God. Thus, the Ten Commandments begin by establishing the primary, "vertical" boundaries that define and protect this sacred relationship. They are not arbitrary rules, but the essential guardrails that keep our hearts rightly oriented toward our Creator.

Based on the Augustinian enumeration of the commandments, the first commandment declares, "You shall have no other gods before me. You shall not make for yourself an idol" (Exodus 20:3-4). This is the foundational boundary of worship. God is establishing exclusivity. In a world filled with countless deities representing every imaginable force of nature and human desire, the God of Israel declares that He alone is worthy of worship. This is not the demand of an insecure egomaniac; it is the protective plea of a loving husband to his bride. An idol is anything we place at the center of our lives other than God—be it wealth, success, family, or even our own comfort. When we worship idols, we give our hearts away to things that can never truly satisfy and will ultimately enslave us all over again. This first boundary is a loving "no" to all lesser gods, so that we can give a wholehearted "yes" to the only One who can give us true life and freedom. It protects our hearts from being divided and ultimately broken.

The second commandment, "You shall not take the name of the LORD your God in vain" (Exodus 20:7), is a boundary on our speech. This goes far beyond just avoiding curse words. To take God's name in vain means to empty it of its weight, to treat it lightly, or to attach it to something that is unholy. It's about protecting the character and reputation of God. When we claim to be followers of God but live in ways that are dishonest, hateful, or unjust, we are taking His name in vain. We are misrepresenting Him to the world. This commandment sets a limit on our hypocrisy. It calls us to a life of integrity, where our words and our actions are aligned and bring honor, not shame, to the name of the One we claim to serve.

The third commandment is perhaps the most radical and counter-cultural boundary of all: "Remember the Sabbath day, to keep it holy" (Exodus 20:8). In a world—both ancient and modern—that is driven by productivity, accumulation, and the ceaseless hum of work, God commands His people to stop. For one full day out of seven, they were to cease from all their labor. This was not a suggestion; it was a command. This is a profound boundary on our striving. The Sabbath is a weekly declaration that our worth is not determined by what we produce. It is a tangible act of trust, acknowledging that God is the ultimate provider and that the world will not fall apart if we take a day to rest. It is a "no" to the tyranny of the urgent, a "no" to the demands of the market, and a "no" to the lie that we are in control. In its place, it is a "yes" to restoration, a "yes" to worship, and a "yes" to delighting in God and His creation. This boundary protects us from burnout, from the idolatry of work, and from the anxiety that comes from relentless self-reliance.

These commandments are the pillars of a healthy relationship with God. They set the limits that allow intimacy and trust to flourish, protecting us from the chaos of idolatry, hypocrisy, and exhaustion.

Horizontal Boundaries: Loving Your Neighbor as Yourself

Once the vertical relationship with God is established, the Law turns to the "horizontal" plane: our relationships with one another. The final command-ments are the non-negotiable boundaries that make community possible. They are the essential "no's" that protect the life, dignity, and property of every person, creating a society where people can feel safe and valued.

The fourth commandment, "Honor your father and your mother" (Exodus 20:12), establishes a boundary of respect within the most fundamental unit of society: the family. It sets a limit on youthful arrogance and rebellion, calling for an attitude of honor toward those who gave us life and nurtured us. This creates a culture of generational respect and ensures the stable transmission of wisdom and values.

The next three commandments are the bedrock of civilization: "You shall not murder... You shall not commit adultery... You shall not steal" (Exodus 20:13-15). These are absolute boundaries protecting the three things most essential to a person's security: their life, their marriage, and their property. Murder is the ultimate violation of a person's physical boundary. Adultery is the ultimate violation of the sacred covenant of marriage. Stealing is the violation of a person's right to the fruit of their labor. Without these basic protections, a society descends into chaos, fear, and violence. They are God's clear declaration that every person has a right to their own life, their own family, and their own possessions, and that these boundaries are not to be crossed.

The eighth commandment, "You shall not bear false witness against your neighbor" (Exodus 20:16), sets a boundary on our words in the context of community. It protects a person's reputation and ensures the possibility of justice. Lies, slander, and gossip can destroy a person as surely as a physical weapon. This commandment creates a society where truth is valued and people are protected from verbal assault.

Finally, the nineth and tenth commandments delves deeper than any of the others, moving from external actions to our internal desires: "You shall not covet" (Exodus 20:17). This is a boundary for the heart. To covet is to have a grasping, obsessive desire for something that is not yours, whether it is your neighbor's house, spouse, or possessions. This commandment gets to the root of the sins listed before it. Murder often begins with coveting someone's life. Adultery begins with coveting someone's spouse. Stealing begins with coveting someone's property. By setting a boundary on our desires, God is teaching us to find contentment in His provision. He is protecting us from the poison of envy and the restless dissatisfaction that destroys our peace and our relationships.

The Ten Commandments, taken together, are a masterpiece of relational design. They are the loving limits that create a safe space for a community to flourish in freedom, protected from chaos both from without and from within.

The Wisdom of Personal Boundaries: A City Without Walls

If the Law provides the grand, societal boundaries, the book of Proverbs offers the practical, personal wisdom for maintaining them. The proverbs are filled with guidance on the importance of self-control, which is the engine of all personal boundary-setting. The most powerful image for this is found in Proverbs 25:28: "A man without self-control is like a city broken into and left without walls."

In the ancient world, a city's walls were its primary source of security and identity. The walls protected the citizens from enemy armies, wild animals, and wandering marauders. They defined the city, marking the boundary between the order and safety within and the chaos and danger without. A city without walls was completely vulnerable. It had no defense, no integrity, no way to protect its resources or its people. It was, for all intents and purposes, no longer a city, but just a collection of exposed and terrified people waiting for disaster.

This is the picture the proverb paints of a person who lacks internal boundaries. They are defenseless against the external attacks of temptation and the internal chaos of their own impulses. Their life is a constant state of crisis management, reacting to every whim, desire, and external pressure.

Consider the "breaches" in the wall that Proverbs warns us about. There is the breach of an uncontrolled tongue. "Death and life are in the power of the tongue" (Proverbs 18:21). A person who cannot set a boundary on their speech, who engages in gossip, slander, and angry outbursts, leaves themselves and their relationships in ruins. They are like a city whose gates are left wide open for enemy spies and saboteurs to enter at will.

There is the breach of uncontrolled appetites. Proverbs warns repeatedly against gluttony and drunkenness, which lead to poverty and ruin (Proverbs 23:21). When we have no boundaries on our consumption—whether of food, drink, media, or material goods—we become enslaved to our appetites. We are a city plundered of its own resources, left weak and impoverished.

There is the breach of uncontrolled anger. "Whoever is slow to anger is better than the mighty, and he who rules his spirit than he who takes a city" (Proverbs 16:32). An uncontrolled temper is a devastating internal enemy. It breaks down relationships, destroys trust, and makes wise decision-making impossible. A person ruled by anger is like a city engaged in a constant civil war, destroying itself from the inside out.

The wisdom of Proverbs is clear: a flourishing life requires strong internal walls. It requires the self-control to say "no" to our own destructive impulses, to set limits on our words, our desires, and our emotions. This is not a call to joyless abstinence, but a call to wise self-governance. It is the path to a life of strength, integrity, and peace—a well-defended city, safe and secure.

Conclusion: A Framework for Flourishing

The Old Testament, far from being a book of life-crushing restrictions, provides us with God's own blueprint for a life of ordered liberty. Through the Law, He gives us the non-negotiable relational boundaries needed for a healthy community. Through the wisdom of Proverbs, He teaches us to build the internal boundaries of self-control that are necessary to maintain that health. These are not burdens to be endured, but gifts to be embraced. They are the loving instructions of our Creator, showing us how to live in the freedom He won for us.

These boundaries are the framework upon which a life of love can be built—love for God, protected by the boundaries of worship and reverence, and love for our neighbor, protected by the boundaries of respect and justice. They teach us that true love is not a boundary-less, sentimental feeling that says "yes" to everything. True love is discerning. It is protective. It is strong enough to say "no" to anything that would harm our relationship with God or with others. It is this profound understanding of a bounded, holy love that is perfectly and beautifully fulfilled in the life of the one to whom the entire Old Testament points: Jesus Christ.

Reflection Questions:

1. Which of the Ten Commandments do you tend to view as an outdated rule, and how might reframing it as a loving, relational boundary change your perspective?

2. The Sabbath was God's gift of a boundary on work. In our 24/7 culture, what would it look like for you to build a "Sabbath" boundary into your life to protect yourself from burnout and to practice trusting God?

3. Consider the metaphor of being a "city without walls" from Proverbs 25:28. In what area of your life (your tongue, your temper, your appetites, your use of time) do you feel most vulnerable or "broken into"? What is one small "wall" you could start building this week?

4. The ninth and tenth commandments set boundaries on our desires ("You shall not covet"). How does the modern world of advertising and social media actively encourage us to cross this boundary? What is one practical step you can take to cultivate contentment?

A Prayer for Loving Limits

Lord God, thank you for the gift of your Law, a framework of love designed for my flourishing. Forgive me for the times I have seen your commands as a burden rather than a blessing. Grant me a heart that loves your boundaries. Teach me to honor the limits you have set for my relationship with You and with others. Holy Spirit, give me the strength to build the walls of self-control in my own heart, that I might rule my spirit well and live a life of integrity and peace. Help me to love

You and my neighbor not with a weak and boundary-less acceptance, but with a strong, discerning, and holy love. Amen.

Chapter Three

The Example of Christ: When Jesus Said No

For the sincere follower of Christ, this is where the rubber truly meets the road. We have seen that God the Father is a God of boundaries, from the creation of the cosmos to the giving of the Law. But we are called to be imitators of Christ. We look to Jesus as our perfect example, the embodiment of love, the one who "did not come to be served, but to serve, and to give His life a ransom for many" (Matthew 20:28). And in that beautiful, self-giving example, a tension can arise. If Jesus's life was one of constant service and sacrifice, how can we, his followers, justify saying "no"? Doesn't a life of love mean a life of limitless, boundary-less giving?

This is perhaps the most significant hurdle for Christians to overcome in embracing a healthy, bounded life. We have a holy desire to be like Jesus, but we often carry a caricature of him in our minds: a Jesus who was available to everyone, 24/7, who never got tired, never felt overwhelmed, and never turned anyone away. We picture him as a divine vending machine of healing and help, and we feel that we, too, should be endlessly available to meet the needs of everyone around us. To say "no," then, can feel like a profound spiritual failure, a direct contradiction of the example of our Savior.

But a careful reading of the Gospels reveals a very different picture. Jesus Christ, the perfect embodiment of love, was also a master of setting boundaries. He did not live a frantic, reactive life, pulled in a thousand directions by the demands of the crowd. He lived a focused, intentional, and purposeful life, and that required him to say "no" just as strategically as he said "yes." His boundaries were not a contradiction to his love; they were the very framework that protected his mission of love. He knew that to give his ultimate "yes" at the cross, he had to say many "no's" along the way. If we truly want to be like Jesus, we must study not only his compassion, but also his courage—the courage to set limits, to protect his priorities, and to stay focused on the will of His Father above all else.

The Boundary of Solitude: Protecting the Source

One of the most consistent patterns we see in Jesus's life is his practice of strategic withdrawal. At the very moments when his popularity was surging and the demands on him were at their peak, Jesus would intentionally step away from the noise of the crowd to be alone with his Father. This was not an act of selfish introversion; it was an act of spiritual necessity. He was protecting his most vital relationship, the very source of his power and authority.

A powerful example of this is found in the first chapter of Mark's Gospel. Jesus has just begun his public ministry in Capernaum, and it is an explosive success. He has taught with authority in the synagogue, cast out a demon, healed Simon's mother-in-law, and then, as the sun set, it seems the entire city showed up at his door. Mark tells us that "the whole city was gathered at the door. And He healed many who were ill with various diseases, and cast out many demons" (Mark 1:33-34).

Imagine the scene. The energy, the excitement, the desperation. This is the moment a modern ministry strategist would dream of. The movement is going viral. The crowds are massive. The needs are endless. The logical next step would be to capitalize on the momentum—set up a healing tent, organize the disciples, and work through the night. The needs were legitimate, and Jesus had the power to meet them.

But what does Jesus do? "In the early morning, while it was still dark, Jesus got up, left the house, and went away to a secluded place, and was praying there" (Mark 1:35).

This is a radical act of boundary-setting. Jesus says "no" to the crowd. He says "no" to the endless, pressing needs. He says "no" to the momentum of his own ministry. Why? So he could say "yes" to his Father. He knew that his ability to give to the people was directly dependent on what he received from the Father in solitude. His public ministry was fueled by his private communion.

The story continues when his disciples, waking up to find the crowds already gathering again, panic. "Simon and his companions searched for Him; they found Him, and said to Him, 'Everyone is looking for You'" (Mark 1:36-37). Notice the subtle pressure in their words. "Everyone is looking for you!" They are communicating the expectations of the crowd. They are, in effect, saying, "You can't be out here praying! You have to get back to work. People need you."

Jesus's response is stunning. He does not apologize. He does not rush back to meet the demand. Instead, he reasserts his own mission, a mission clarified in his time of prayer. "Let us go somewhere else to the towns nearby, so that I may preach there also; for that is what I came for" (Mark 1:38). His time with the Father had reminded him of his primary purpose. He was not just a healer; he was a preacher of the good news. He refused to let the crowd's agenda—even their legitimate need for healing—derail his God-given purpose.

This pattern is repeated throughout the Gospels. Luke 5:15-16 tells us, "But the news about Him was spreading even more, and large crowds were gathering to hear Him and to be healed of their sicknesses. But Jesus Himself would often slip away to the wilderness and pray." The word "often" is key. This was not a one-time event; it was a regular discipline. The more the demands of the ministry grew, the more intentional Jesus became about setting a boundary of solitude.

What does this teach us? It gives us divine permission to protect our own source. If Jesus, the perfect Son of God, needed to say "no" to people in order to say "yes" to prayer, how much more do we? We live in a culture that glorifies busyness and constant availability. We are tethered to devices that make us accessible 24/7. But Jesus shows us that spiritual health and sustainable ministry require us to build a wall around our time with God. It means having the courage to turn off the phone, to close the laptop, to let a non-urgent email wait, and to say to the legitimate demands of the world, "Not right now. This time is for my Father."

The Boundary of Identity: Resisting the Temptation to Compromise

If Jesus's withdrawal to the wilderness shows us a boundary for the sake of relationship, his temptation in the wilderness shows us a boundary for the sake of identity. In Matthew 4, after forty days of fasting, Jesus is at his weakest physically. It is at this moment that Satan comes to attack him at the level of his core identity, which had just been affirmed at his baptism: "This is My beloved Son, in whom I am well-pleased" (Matthew 3:17). Each of the three temptations is a subtle and insidious attempt to get Jesus to act outside of that identity as the trusting, obedient Son.

The first temptation is an attack on his dependence. "If You are the Son of God, command that these stones become bread" (Matthew 4:3). Satan is not tempting Jesus to do something inherently sinful. Making bread is not a sin, and Jesus is hungry. It is a legitimate need. But the temptation is to use his divine power for his own provision, to operate independently of the Father's timing and will. It is a temptation to take a shortcut. Jesus's response is a firm "no," grounded in Scripture: "It is written, 'Man shall not live on bread alone, but on every word that proceeds out of the mouth of God.'" He sets a boundary, refusing to use his power to meet a legitimate need in an illegitimate way. He chooses dependence on the Father over self-reliance.

The second temptation is an attack on his trust. Satan takes him to the highest point of the temple and says, "If You are the Son of God, throw Yourself down; for it is written, 'He will command His angels concerning You'" (Matthew 4:6). This is a temptation to test God, to force His hand and create a public spectacle to prove his identity. It's a temptation to manipulate God for a dramatic result.

Again, Jesus responds with a boundary-setting "no," quoting Scripture: "On the other hand, it is written, 'You shall not put the Lord your God to the test.'" He refuses to step outside the bounds of a trusting relationship with his Father. He will not treat God as a cosmic genie to be summoned for a magic show.

The third temptation is the most direct attack on his worship. Satan shows him all the kingdoms of the world and says, "All these things I will give You, if You fall down and worship me" (Matthew 4:9). This is the ultimate shortcut. Satan offers Jesus the very thing he came to win—lordship over all nations—but without the suffering of the cross. The price is simple: a momentary act of compromised worship. Jesus's response is his most forceful "no" yet: "Go, Satan! For it is written, 'You shall worship the Lord your God, and serve Him only.'" He draws the non-negotiable boundary of worship. His allegiance is to the Father alone, and he will not compromise it for anything, not even for the prize of the whole world.

In these three powerful refusals, Jesus teaches us that boundaries are essential for protecting our identity and our mission. Satan will always tempt us to take shortcuts, to meet legitimate needs in illegitimate ways, to test God's faithfulness, and to compromise our worship for the promise of an easier path. A life of integrity requires us to have a firm, scripture-based "no" at the ready. It means saying "no" to the business deal that requires a little dishonesty. It means saying "no" to the relationship that would pull us away from our devotion to God. It means saying "no" to the allure of popularity if it requires us to soften the truth of the gospel. These boundaries protect our very soul.

The Boundary of Purpose: Refusing a Lesser Kingdom

Perhaps one of the most challenging boundaries to set is the one against good things that are not the best things. It is relatively easy to say "no" to obvious sin. It is much harder to say "no" to a good opportunity that is simply not the right one for us. Jesus provides a powerful example of this after one of his most spectacular miracles.

In John 6, Jesus has just fed a crowd of over five thousand people with only five barley loaves and two fish. The people are astounded. Their stomachs are full, and their minds are racing. They have been waiting for a Messiah who would be a political and military leader, one who would overthrow their Roman oppressors and restore the earthly kingdom of Israel. In their eyes, anyone who can miraculously create food to feed an army is the perfect candidate. Their response is immediate and decisive: they intend "to come and take Him by force to make Him king" (John 6:15).

Let's pause and appreciate the magnitude of this offer. This is not a temptation from Satan in the wilderness; this is a grassroots movement of the people. They want to give him power, honor, and a throne. This is a good thing, right? It would give him a platform to do so much good. And yet, what is Jesus's response? He says "no." He doesn't just politely decline; he perceives their intent and "withdrew again to the mountain by Himself alone." He physically removes himself from the situation. He sets a hard boundary against their agenda.

Why? Because their kingdom was not the kingdom he came to build. They wanted a political king who would fill their bellies and fight their battles. Jesus came to be a suffering servant who would save their souls and conquer sin and death. Their agenda, while well-intentioned from their perspective, was a distraction from his ultimate purpose. Accepting their offer would have been a catastrophic mission drift. He had to say "no" to their earthly crown so he could say "yes" to the Father's thorny one.

This is a profound lesson for every Christian. We will be presented with many good opportunities in our lives—opportunities to serve on committees, to lead projects, to join movements. Many of them will be good, honorable, and kingdom-minded things. But not every good thing is a God thing for us. We each have a unique calling and a limited amount of time, energy, and resources. Like Jesus, we must have a clear sense of our God-given purpose, a purpose that is clarified in our times of solitude with the Father. And with that clarity, we must have the courage to say "no" to good opportunities that would distract us from the best one to which God has called us. This is not selfish; it is wise stewardship. It is choosing to do a few things well for the glory of God, rather than doing many things poorly out of a fear of missing out.

Conclusion: The Courage of a Christ-like "No"

The life of Christ, when we look closely, is not a model for a frantic, boundary-less existence. It is a model for a focused, centered, and deeply purposeful life. Jesus's "no" was never arbitrary, selfish, or unkind. It was always a strategic and loving act of protection.

He set boundaries to protect his relationship with the Father, the source of his life and power. He set boundaries to protect his identity as the obedient Son, refusing to compromise his integrity. He set boundaries to protect his purpose, refusing to be distracted by lesser agendas. He honored his own human limits, embracing rest and teaching his disciples to do the same.

To follow the example of Christ is not to become a doormat for the demands of the world. It is to live with the same holy intentionality that he did. It means cultivating the courage to say "no" to the crowd so we can say "yes" to the Father. It means saying "no" to compromise so we can say "yes" to our identity in him. It means saying "no" to good distractions so we can give our wholehearted "yes" to our unique, God-given calling.

This is a radical and counter-cultural way to live. But it is the path of true freedom and fruitfulness. It is the path that our Savior walked, and he invites us to walk it with him.

Reflection Questions:

1. In what ways have you allowed the "tyranny of the urgent" and the needs of others to crowd out your own time for solitude and prayer with the Father? What is one practical boundary you could set this week to protect that time?

2. Reflect on the three temptations of Christ. What are the primary "short-cuts" you are tempted to take in your life—in your career, your relation-

ships, or your spiritual walk? What scriptural truth could you use to set a boundary against that temptation?

3. Can you think of a "good opportunity" you said "yes" to that ended up distracting you from a more important, God-given priority? How can the example of Jesus in John 6 give you the courage to evaluate future opportunities more carefully?

4. Jesus often withdrew when he was most in demand. When are you most likely to neglect your own need for rest and spiritual renewal? How can you plan ahead to set a boundary for rest during those busy seasons?

A Prayer for Christ-like Courage

Lord Jesus, thank you for being my perfect example in all things. Forgive me for creating a version of you in my mind that was endlessly available, and for placing that impossible burden on myself. Thank you for showing me that a life of love is also a life of wise boundaries. Grant me the courage to follow your example. Help me to say "no" to the demands that would pull me away from the Father. Help me to say "no" to the temptations that would compromise my identity in You. Help me to say "no" to the distractions that would derail my purpose. Fill me with your Spirit, that I might live with the same focus, intention, and love that you did, for the glory of God the Father. Amen.

Chapter Four

The Fear Factor: Saying No to the Fear of Man

We have now laid a firm foundation. We have seen that boundaries are not a worldly concept but a divine principle, woven into the fabric of creation, codified in the Law of Love, and perfectly modeled in the life of Jesus Christ. The logic is sound. The biblical precedent is clear. So why is it still so terrifyingly difficult to say "no"? Why do our palms sweat, our hearts race, and our minds flood with a thousand reasons to backtrack when we are faced with a simple request we know we should decline? Why does a two-letter word feel like it weighs a thousand pounds on our tongue?

The reason, for so many of us, is not a lack of theological understanding, but the presence of a deep and powerful emotion: fear. We are not afraid that setting a boundary is wrong in God's eyes; we are afraid of how it will be perceived in the eyes of others. We are afraid of the fallout—the disappointment, the disapproval, the conflict, the potential rejection. This is the heart of the matter, the core obstacle that stands between our intellectual assent to the idea of boundaries and our ability to live a bounded life. The Bible has a name for this condition. It is the "fear of man."

The book of Proverbs, with its characteristic pithy wisdom, puts it plainly: "The fear of man lays a snare, but whoever trusts in the LORD is safe" (Proverbs 29:25). This single verse brilliantly captures the dynamic at play. The fear of man is not just a minor character flaw; it is a snare. A snare is a trap. It is something that looks harmless but is designed to entangle, immobilize, and ultimately destroy its victim. It promises safety—the safety of being liked, of fitting in, of avoiding conflict—but it delivers bondage. The only true path to safety and freedom, the proverb tells us, is to transfer our trust from the fickle opinions of people to the unwavering character of God.

This chapter is about learning to recognize the snare. We will diagnose the subtle and overt ways the fear of man manifests in our lives, explore its devastating spiritual consequences, and then, most importantly, discover the biblical antidote: a right and reverential fear of the Lord that sets us free.

Diagnosing the Snare: What the Fear of Man Looks Like

The fear of man is a chameleon. It rarely shows up in our internal monologue with the straightforward label, "I am afraid of what they will think." Instead, it disguises itself in more noble-sounding language. It masquerades as kindness, humility, and a servant's heart. To escape the snare, we must learn to identify its various forms.

One of its most common disguises is people-pleasing. A people-pleaser is driven by an insatiable need for approval. Their sense of well-being rises and falls with the opinions of others. They feel a compulsive need to make everyone happy, and they experience any form of disapproval as a personal failure. For the people-pleaser, saying "no" feels like a direct assault on their core identity, which is built on being seen as helpful, agreeable, and nice. Their "yes" is often not a genuine expression of love or capacity, but a desperate bid for validation. They are trying to earn an acceptance that, in Christ, they already possess.

Another form of this fear is conflict avoidance, or what might be called "peace-faking." This person is not necessarily seeking applause, but they are terrified of discord. The mere possibility of a disagreement, a tense conversation, or someone being upset with them is enough to trigger a compliant "yes." They will agree to things they don't have time for, take on responsibilities that aren't theirs, and remain silent when they should speak up, all to maintain a fragile, superficial peace. They mistake the absence of conflict for the presence of true shalom. But a faked peace is no peace at all; it is simply suppressed resentment and unresolved tension that will inevitably fester and explode. A boundary, spoken in love, is an act of peace-making, not peace-faking. It brings truth to the surface so that a real, authentic relationship can be built.

A deeper, more primal form of this fear is the fear of rejection or abandonment. For those who have experienced relational trauma or insecurity, the thought of someone pulling away from them is unbearable. They say "yes" as a form of relationship insurance. Their compliance is a way of saying, "Please don't leave me. See how useful I am? See how indispensable I am? You need me." They use their service as a way to secure their place in a family, a friend group, or a church, living with the constant, low-grade anxiety that if they stop performing, they will be cast aside.

Finally, there is the fear of being misunderstood or mislabeled. This is especially potent in Christian circles. We are afraid that if we say "no" to a request at church, we will be labeled as "uncommitted." If we set a boundary with a struggling friend, we will be labeled as "uncompassionate." If we decline to take on an extra project at work, we will be labeled as "not a team player." These labels threaten our reputation and our sense of belonging. To avoid them, we overload our schedules, neglect our families, and burn ourselves out, all to maintain a carefully curated public image that may have little to do with our actual, God-given calling.

Do you see yourself in any of these descriptions? The truth is, most of us have felt the pull of these fears at some point. They are a common part of our fallen human experience. But to live in them, to allow them to be the primary motivator of our decisions, is to be caught in a snare that will choke out our spiritual vitality.

The Spiritual Consequences of the Snare

Living in the fear of man is not a neutral state; it is spiritually corrosive. It slowly eats away at the foundations of our faith and leads to a life of quiet desperation and ineffectiveness.

First, as the Apostle Paul so clearly understood, it creates a divided loyalty. He asks the Galatian church a piercing question: "For am I now seeking the approval of man, or of God? Or am I trying to please man? If I were still trying to please man, I would not be a servant of Christ" (Galatians 1:10). The logic is inescapable. You cannot have two ultimate masters. You cannot make pleasing God your highest goal while simultaneously making pleasing people your highest goal. At some point, these two agendas will conflict. The crowd will demand one thing, and Christ will demand another. The fear of man will always tempt you to choose the crowd. It will cause you to soften the truth of the gospel, to laugh at the inappropriate joke, to remain silent in the face of injustice. As Paul states, a people-pleaser cannot be a true servant of Christ, because their ultimate allegiance is to the shifting opinions of their audience, not to the unchanging truth of their King.

Second, the fear of man leads to spiritual exhaustion. Trying to meet the endless and often contradictory expectations of everyone around you is a recipe for burnout. It is an impossible task. You are trying to fill a bucket with a hole in it, seeking to get enough approval to finally feel secure, but the validation never lasts. This leads to a life of frantic, joyless activity, rather than a life of peaceful, purposeful service. We end up giving from a place of emptiness and anxiety, rather than from the overflow of a heart filled with the love of God. The result is often resentment. We begin to resent the very people we are trying so hard to please, because our service is not a free gift, but a transaction that is failing to deliver the promised reward of acceptance.

Finally, the fear of man robs us of the peace and joy that are our birthright in Christ. The one who trusts in the Lord is "safe," says the proverb. This safety is a deep, soul-level peace that comes from knowing you are unconditionally loved and accepted by the only one whose opinion truly matters. When you live for an audience of One, you are liberated from the tyranny of the crowd. You can make decisions based on conviction rather than compulsion. You can serve freely and joyfully, knowing that your worth is not on the line. The fear of man keeps us in a state of constant, low-grade anxiety, always monitoring the reactions of others, always adjusting our performance. It is a life of bondage, a far cry from the glorious freedom of the children of God.

The Antidote: The Fear of the Lord

If the fear of man is the snare, the fear of the Lord is the key that unlocks it. The Bible consistently presents these two fears as mutually exclusive. The more your heart is filled with a right fear of God, the less room there will be for the fear of man.

But what is the "fear of the Lord"? It is crucial that we understand this correctly. It is not the cowering terror of a slave before a cruel master. It is not a neurotic anxiety about making a mistake and being struck by lightning. The biblical fear of the Lord is a rich, multifaceted concept that is best understood as reverential awe. It is the breathtaking, heart-in-your-throat wonder you feel when you stand on the edge of the Grand Canyon. It is the overwhelming sense of smallness and reverence you feel when you gaze up at a star-filled night sky. It is the recognition that you are in the presence of someone so magnificent, so powerful, so holy, and so loving that all other concerns fade into insignificance.

To fear the Lord is to have your life reoriented around His reality. It is to see Him as He is—the sovereign Creator, the righteous Judge, the merciful Redeemer—and to see yourself as you are in relation to Him. When you are rightly captivated by the majesty of God, the opinions of people are put in their proper perspective. What is the disapproval of your boss compared to the smile of your Creator? What is the awkwardness of a difficult conversation compared to the peace of knowing you are walking in obedience to the King of the universe?

This is the freedom that Daniel experienced when he chose to pray to God, even when a royal decree made it a capital offense. His fear of God was greater than his fear of the lions' den (Daniel 6). It is the freedom that Shadrach, Meshach, and Abednego felt when they stood before King Nebuchadnezzar and declared, "If we are thrown into the blazing furnace, the God we serve is able to deliver us... But even if He does not... we will not serve your gods" (Daniel 3:17-18). Their fear of God was greater than their fear of the fire. It is the freedom that Peter and John experienced when they stood before the Sanhedrin, the most powerful religious body of their day, and were commanded to stop speaking about Jesus. Their response was a masterclass in the fear of the Lord: "Whether it is right in the sight of God to listen to you rather than to God, you must judge" (Acts 4:19). Their fear of God was greater than their fear of the authorities.

In each case, a greater fear displaced a lesser one. Awe of God conquered anxiety about man. This is the only lasting solution. You cannot simply will yourself to stop caring what people think. You must be so overwhelmed by what God thinks that the opinions of others lose their gravitational pull on your heart.

From Snare to Safety: Practical Steps

How do we cultivate this holy fear? How do we move from the snare of people-pleasing to the safety of trusting God? It is a lifelong journey, but it begins with intentional, practical steps.

First, you must root your identity in Christ. The fear of man thrives in the soil of an insecure identity. As long as you are looking to other people to tell you who you are, you will be their slave. You must, through daily prayer and meditation on Scripture, consciously reject the labels the world offers and embrace the identity God has given you. You are a beloved child of God (1 John 3:1). You are chosen, holy, and dearly loved (Colossians 3:12). You were bought with a price (1 Corinthians 6:20). Your worth is not based on your performance, your productivity, or your popularity. It was sealed at the cross, and it is non-negotiable. Rehearsing these truths day after day is not just positive thinking; it is spiritual warfare against the lies that fuel the fear of man.

Second, you must practice small acts of courage. Overcoming a deep-seated fear is like building a muscle. You don't start by trying to lift the heaviest weight in the gym. You start with something manageable and build strength over time. If the thought of saying "no" to your boss or your mother-in-law is overwhelming, start smaller. Say "no" to the store clerk who asks if you want to sign up for a credit card. Politely decline a social invitation you don't have the energy for. State a differing opinion in a low-stakes conversation. Each time you act with courage, no matter how small, you are rewiring your brain. You are teaching yourself that you can survive disapproval, that the world does not end when someone is unhappy with your decision. You are building your "courage muscle" for the bigger challenges ahead.

Finally, you must redefine your goal. The goal of your life is not to be liked; it is to be faithful. It is not to be popular; it is to be obedient. It is not to keep everyone happy; it is to please the Lord. This requires a conscious shift in your internal scorecard. At the end of the day, instead of asking, "Did everyone like me today?" ask, "Was I faithful to what God called me to do today?" This changes everything. It reframes your decisions around a new and singular purpose. When faithfulness to God is your goal, setting a boundary is no longer a relational risk; it is an act of worship.

Overcoming the fear of man is not about becoming a callous or uncaring person. It is about becoming so secure in God's love that you are free to love others authentically, not out of a desperate need for their approval, but out of a genuine desire for their good. It is the path from the snare to safety, from bondage to freedom, from a life of fear to a life of faith.

Reflection Questions:

1. In which of the disguises of the "fear of man" do you most often see yourself (people-pleasing, conflict avoidance, fear of rejection, fear of being mislabeled)? Be specific and honest.

2. Galatians 1:10 presents a stark choice between pleasing man and serving Christ. Can you think of a recent situation where you felt this tension? Which did you choose, and why?

3. What does the "fear of the Lord" mean to you in a practical sense? How is it different from simply being afraid of God's punishment? What is one thing you could do this week to cultivate a greater sense of awe and

reverence for God?

4. Of the three practical steps (rooting your identity, practicing small acts of courage, redefining your goal), which one feels most needed and most achievable for you in your current season of life? What is one small step you can take in that area?

A Prayer for Holy Fear

Father in Heaven, I confess that I have been caught in the snare of the fear of man. I have elevated the opinions of others above Your opinion of me. I have sought approval from people more than I have sought to be faithful to You. Forgive me. Lord, replace my fear of man with a right and holy fear of You. Captivate my heart with Your majesty, Your power, and Your incredible love for me. Let my awe of You be so great that the approval and disapproval of others fade into the background. Root my identity so deeply in Your love that I no longer need to perform for my worth. Grant me the courage to be faithful, not popular. Make me a servant of Christ alone. Amen.

Chapter Five

The Guilt Complex: Saying No to False Responsibility

I f the fear of man is the external pressure that traps us in a cycle of unwanted "yeses," then guilt is its internal accomplice. Fear and guilt are two sides of the same counterfeit coin, both passed off as genuine servants of love but in reality, cruel masters of obligation. Fear asks, "What will they think of me?" Guilt whispers, "What kind of person are you if you don't help?" While fear is preoccupied with the future consequences of a "no," guilt weaponizes the present moment, attacking our character and convincing us that setting a boundary is a moral failure. For many Christians, this guilt complex is an even more formidable obstacle than the fear of man.

We are a people called to love, to serve, to be compassionate, and to care for the needy. These are beautiful, non-negotiable commands. But our enemy is a master of twisting good things into destructive ones. He takes our genuine, Spirit-given desire to help and overlays it with a crushing, unbiblical sense of responsibility for everyone and everything. We begin to operate under a set of unspoken, unholy rules: If there is a need, I am responsible for meeting it. If someone is struggling, I am responsible for fixing it. If someone is unhappy, I am responsible for making them happy.

This mindset, though it may feel righteous, is a fast track to burnout, resentment, and a profoundly ineffective Christian life. It transforms the joy of Spirit-led service into the drudgery of guilt-driven servitude. To break free, we must learn to differentiate between the Holy Spirit's true conviction and the heavy yoke of false guilt. We must understand the critical biblical distinction between bearing a burden and carrying a load, for in that distinction lies the freedom to say "no" not just with courage, but with a clear and peaceful conscience.

The Weight of the World: When Responsibility Becomes an Idol

Where does this false guilt come from? Often, it stems from an over-inflated sense of our own importance and responsibility—a subtle form of pride that masquerades as humility. We see a problem and immediately assume we are the solution. We inadvertently place ourselves in the role of savior, rushing in to rescue people from the consequences of their own choices, their financial mismanagement, or their emotional immaturity. We believe, deep down, that if we don't step in, disaster will strike, and it will be our fault.

This is a savior complex, and it is a heavy burden to bear because the role is already taken. There is only one Savior, and it is not us. When we take on the responsibility for fixing everyone's life, we are trying to do God's job, and we are not qualified for the position. This leads to a life where we are constantly trying to manage the unmanageable, control the uncontrollable, and change the unchangeable.

The result is a life lived in reaction to crises rather than in obedience to a calling. Our schedule is not our own; it belongs to the most demanding or irresponsible person in our life at that moment. Our resources are not stewarded; they are hemorrhaged in a series of bailouts. Our emotional energy is not invested; it is drained by the constant drama of others. We become enablers, inadvertently funding the addiction, excusing the irresponsibility, and cleaning up the messes that God, in His wisdom, may be using to bring someone to a place of repentance and maturity.

False guilt feels heavy, condemning, and frantic. It pressures you to act immediately, without prayer or counsel. It whispers that your worth is tied to your usefulness. In contrast, the Holy Spirit's conviction is peaceful, specific, and freeing.

It doesn't condemn your character; it invites you to participate in a specific act of love that God has prepared for you. Learning to tell the difference between these two voices is the first step toward freedom.

The Key to Freedom: Burdens vs. Loads in Galatians 6

The Apostle Paul, with his brilliant pastoral insight, provides the single most helpful passage in all of Scripture for dismantling the guilt complex. In his letter to the Galatians, he appears at first to give a contradictory command. But in this apparent contradiction, we find a perfectly balanced and liberating truth.

He begins in verse 2: "Bear one another's burdens, and so fulfill the law of Christ" (Galatians 6:2).

This is the verse that people with a guilt complex have memorized. It is the banner under which they march into a life of over-commitment. To "bear one another's burdens" sounds like an all-encompassing command to help anyone with any problem at any time. But the Greek word used here for "burdens" is baros. It refers to a crushing, oppressive weight—a load that is too heavy for one person to carry alone. Think of a boulder that has pinned someone to the ground. This is not about the daily challenges of life; it is about the catastrophic, overwhelming crises.

This is the friend who receives a devastating medical diagnosis. This is the family whose house has just burned down. This is the person deep in the throes of grief after losing a spouse. These are the baros—the crushing burdens of life. In these moments, the law of Christ, the law of love, compels us to come alongside them. We are to get our shoulder under that boulder with them, to bring meals, to provide comfort, to offer financial help, to weep with those who weep. This is a temporary, crisis-level intervention. It is an all-hands-on-deck, emergency response of love.

However, if Paul had stopped there, he would have left us vulnerable to the guilt complex we are trying to dismantle. But he doesn't. He continues, and in verse 5, he provides the crucial counterbalance: "for each will have to bear his own load" (Galatians 6:5).

At first glance, this seems to contradict what he just said. But Paul uses a different Greek word here. The word for "load" is phortion. This word refers to a person's daily allotment of responsibility. It was the common term for a soldier's backpack or a person's daily cargo. This is not a crushing, abnormal weight; it is the normal, everyday stuff of life that each person is expected to carry for themselves.

Your phortion, your load, includes your job, your budget, your chores, your spiritual disciplines, and the consequences of your own choices. It is the backpack of personal responsibility that God has given to each of us. Paul is saying that while we are called to help each other with the catastrophic burdens, we are each ultimately responsible for carrying our own daily load.

This distinction is the key that unlocks the prison of false guilt. It gives us a biblical framework for discernment. When someone comes to you with a need, you are no longer faced with a simple yes/no dilemma. You are now equipped to ask a new set of questions: Is this a crushing burden (baros) that I am called to help lift? Or is this a daily load (phortion) that they are responsible for carrying themselves?

The Loving "No": Refusing to Carry Someone Else's Backpack

Let's make this practical. A friend calls you in a panic. She has overspent her budget again and can't pay her rent, which is due tomorrow. This feels like a crisis, a heavy burden. Your guilt flares up, telling you that a good Christian friend would write a check. But let's apply the Galatians 6 filter. Is this a baros or a phortion? A sudden job loss or a medical emergency would be a baros. But a consistent pattern of financial mismanagement is a phortion. It is her backpack of daily responsibility that she is asking you to carry for her.

To write the check might feel loving in the short term, but it is actually an act of enabling. You are preventing her from feeling the natural consequences of her choices—the very consequences that might motivate her to learn how to budget, to seek financial counseling, or to trust God more deeply for her provision. Carrying her phortion stunts her growth. A truly loving response would be to say "no" to giving her the money, but "yes" to helping her in a way that empowers her. You might say, "I am so sorry you are in this stressful situation. I am not able to give you money for your rent, but I would love to sit down with you this weekend and help you create a budget, or help you find a good financial counselor." This response honors the boundary. You are refusing to carry her load, but you are offering to help her bear the burden of learning how to carry it herself.

Consider another example. A fellow church member is notoriously disorganized and over-committed. He consistently signs up for things and then, at the last minute, calls you in a panic to finish his part of the project because he has run out of time. This is his phortion. It is his responsibility to manage his own schedule. Every time you say "yes" and rescue him, you are preventing him from learning the crucial life skill of time management and the spiritual discipline of keeping his word. The loving, boundary-setting response is a kind but firm, "I know you are in a tough spot, but I am not able to take that on for you. I have my own commitments to honor."

Saying "no" to carrying someone else's load is not an act of selfishness. It is an act of respect. It communicates, "I believe you are capable of carrying this. I respect you enough not to step in and rob you of the opportunity to grow in strength and responsibility." It is one of the most loving things you can do. It is also an act of wise stewardship of your own life. Every ounce of energy you spend carrying someone else's backpack is energy you cannot invest in carrying your own load well, or in being available for the true baros moments when God genuinely calls you to help.

Letting Go of the Guilt

Freedom from the guilt complex requires a profound shift in our understanding of love. Biblical love (agape) is not about making people feel happy and comfortable at all times. It is about willing the ultimate good for another person. And sometimes, the ultimate good for another person is that they experience the discomfort necessary for growth.

When you set a boundary and refuse to carry someone's load, they may not be happy with you. They may try to manipulate you, calling you selfish or unloving. This is the moment when you must cling to the truth. Your decision was not based on a lack of love, but on a deeper, wiser, and more biblical form of love. Your conscience can be clear before God. You are allowing that person the dignity of their own choices and the opportunity to learn from them.

Letting go of false guilt means entrusting people to God. It means recognizing that you are not their Holy Spirit. It is not your job to convict, to change, or to control them. It is your job to be faithful to what God has called you to do, and to love others with the kind of wisdom that empowers, rather than enables. It is to understand that sometimes, the most compassionate response is a loving, courageous, and guilt-free "no."

Reflection Questions:

1. Think of a recurring situation in your life where you feel a strong sense of guilt or obligation. Is the issue a true, crushing burden (baros) or is it someone's daily load (phortion) that you have taken on?

2. Describe a time when you "rescued" someone from the consequences of their choices. In hindsight, did your help lead to their long-term growth or did it create a cycle of dependency?

3. The chapter suggests that saying "no" can be an act of respect. How does this idea challenge your previous understanding of helping others?

4. When you feel the pang of false guilt, what truth from Scripture can you use to speak back to that feeling? How can you remind yourself that your responsibility is to be faithful, not to be the savior?

A Prayer for a Clear Conscience

Lord, I confess that I have carried the heavy weight of false guilt. I have taken on responsibilities that were never mine to bear, and I have tried to be the savior in situations where only You can save. Forgive me for my pride and my lack of trust in You. Grant me the wisdom to discern between a true burden I am called to bear and a daily load that belongs to another. Give me the courage to say "no" with love and a clear conscience, trusting that You are at work in that person's life in ways I cannot see. Free me from the bondage of guilt, that I might serve You with joy and peace, faithful to the specific loads and burdens You have called me to carry. Amen.

Chapter Six

The Stewardship Mandate: Saying Yes to God's Priorities

U p to this point, our journey has been largely defensive. We have focused on the theology and psychology of saying "no"—building a biblical case for boundaries, learning from the example of Christ, and dismantling the internal obstacles of fear and guilt. We have been learning how to build the walls of our city, how to protect ourselves from the chaos of a boundary-less life. This is essential, foundational work. But a city is more than just its walls. The purpose of the walls is to protect the vibrant, fruitful, and purposeful life happening inside them. The ultimate goal of saying "no" is not to create an empty, protected fortress, but to cultivate a flourishing garden where we can give our best and most focused "yes."

This chapter marks a crucial turning point in our thinking. We will now shift from a defensive posture to an offensive one. We will move from the freedom from a life of obligation to the freedom for a life of purpose. The power of "no" is not an end in itself; it is the strategic tool that makes a life of intentionality possible. Every time you say "no" to a lesser opportunity, you are creating the space, time, and energy to say "yes" to a greater one. Every refusal of a good thing is an embrace of the best thing to which God has called you.

This is the heart of the stewardship mandate. Stewardship is the simple but profound recognition that everything we have—our time, our talents, our energy, our resources, our very next breath—is not our own. It is a sacred trust, a gift on loan from a generous God. And He has entrusted these gifts to us not for our own idle consumption, but for us to invest wisely for His glory and for the good of His kingdom. A life of undisciplined, reactive "yeses" is, therefore, not just a recipe for burnout; it is an act of poor stewardship. It is like taking the precious seeds a master gardener has given you and scattering them carelessly on rocky ground, rather than planting them intentionally in the good soil where they will bear the most fruit.

The Unforgiving Minute: Stewarding Your Finite Resources

The first and most sobering reality of stewardship is that our primary resources are finite. We cannot create more time. We cannot manufacture more energy. The psalmist Moses, in one of the oldest and wisest prayers in the Bible, pleads with God: "So teach us to number our days, that we may get a heart of wisdom" (Psalm 90:12). To "number our days" is to live with an acute awareness of our own mortality and the precious, limited nature of our time on this earth. It is to understand that the clock is always ticking. A heart of wisdom, then, is one that does not squander this non-renewable resource but invests it with purpose.

The Apostle Paul echoes this sentiment with a greater sense of urgency in his letter to the Ephesians. He writes, "Look carefully then how you walk, not as unwise but as wise, making the best use of the time, because the days are evil" (Ephesians 5:15-16). The phrase "making the best use of the time" can be translated as "redeeming the time." It carries the idea of buying something back from the marketplace, of seizing an opportunity before it is gone. Paul is telling us that time is a precious commodity, and the days are filled with evil—that is, with futility, distraction, and things that would steal our time and purpose. The wise person, therefore, is a careful and strategic investor of their time. They don't just let their days happen to them; they happen to their days.

Now, connect this reality to the pressure of a boundary-less life. When you operate without a clear sense of your God-given priorities, you allow your most precious resource—your time—to be dictated by the agendas of others. Your schedule becomes a public commodity, available to the highest bidder of urgency or demand. You give an hour to a pointless meeting, a morning to a task someone else should have done, an evening to a commitment you made out of guilt. Each of these careless "yeses" is a squandering of your sacred trust. You are selling off irreplaceable minutes and hours for the cheap price of avoiding an awkward conversation.

The same is true of our energy. We wake up each morning with a finite amount of physical, emotional, and spiritual energy. A life without boundaries is a life of constant energy leaks. We spend it in draining conversations, in stressful, last-minute scrambles to fulfill unwise commitments, and in the emotional labor of managing everyone's expectations. By midday, our tank is empty, and we have nothing left for the people and the tasks that matter most—our spouse, our children, our time with God, our primary calling. A wise steward understands that their energy is a gift to be invested, not a resource to be squandered. They build boundaries into their life—like the Sabbath rest we saw in Chapter 2—to protect and replenish that energy, so it can be deployed with strength and focus toward their divine priorities.

The Investor's Mindset: Lessons from the Parable of the Talents

If the psalmist and Paul give us the "why" of stewardship (our resources are finite), Jesus, in the Parable of the Talents, gives us the "how." This parable, found in Matthew 25, is not just a story about money; it is the single most important passage in Scripture for understanding a steward's mindset. It is a call to move from a passive, fearful preservation of our gifts to an active, courageous investment of them.

The story is familiar. A master entrusts his property to three servants before he leaves on a long journey. To one, he gives five talents; to another, two; and to another, one, "each according to his ability." A talent was a significant sum of money, worth perhaps twenty years of a laborer's wages. This is no small gift. The first two servants immediately "went and traded with them" and doubled their master's money. The third servant, however, was motivated by fear. He says to the master upon his return, "I was afraid, and I went and hid your talent in the ground." The master's response is scathing. He calls the servant "wicked and slothful" and takes the one talent from him, giving it to the one who has ten.

This parable shatters the idea that faithfulness is about playing it safe. The master did not praise the third servant for not losing the money. He condemned him for not doing anything with it. The only two options in the parable are multiplication or subtraction. There is no middle ground of safe preservation. The master expected a return on his investment.

This is the investor's mindset that God calls us to. He has given each of us a unique portfolio of "talents"—our time, our spiritual gifts, our natural abilities, our experiences, our relationships, our resources. And He has one expectation: that we put them to work to produce a return for His kingdom.

Now, how does this relate to saying "no"? A wise financial investor does not put their money into every possible stock. They research. They discern. They develop a strategy. They say "no" to hundreds of mediocre or speculative investments so they can say a confident "yes" to the few that they believe will yield the greatest return. A boundary-less Christian is like a foolish investor who puts a little bit of money into every single stock they hear about. Their portfolio is a chaotic, unfocused mess, and their returns will be minimal.

A wise Christian steward, on the other hand, prayerfully discerns their primary calling. They ask, "Lord, given the unique portfolio of talents you have given me, where can I invest them to produce the greatest return for Your glory?" They understand that they cannot do everything, so they must choose to do the most important things. This requires the courage to say "no" to dozens of "good" investment opportunities that are simply not the best fit for their unique portfolio. They say "no" to serving in the children's ministry if their gift is administration. They say "no" to leading the small group if their gift is mercy and one-on-one discipleship. They are not being unspiritual; they are being strategic. They are focusing their investment where it will yield the thirty, sixty, or hundredfold return that Jesus talks about in the Parable of the Sower.

Defining Your "Yes": Discovering Your Divine Priorities

This all sounds good in theory, but it begs the practical question: How do I know what my most important "yeses" are? How do I discern my primary, God-given priorities so that I can confidently say "no" to the things that fall outside of them? This is not a formula, but a lifelong process of discovery that involves several key disciplines.

First, it begins with prayer and Scripture. This is non-negotiable. You cannot know the will of the Giver if you do not spend time in conversation with Him. This is why Jesus's practice of solitude, which we explored in Chapter 3, is so vital. It was in those quiet moments with the Father that his mission was clarified and affirmed. We must ask God directly: "Lord, what are the primary things you have called me to in this season of my life? What are the non-negotiables? What are the core responsibilities you have entrusted to my care?" As you marinate your mind in Scripture, the Holy Spirit will begin to illuminate the principles and priorities of the kingdom, giving you a grid through which to evaluate your own life.

Second, you must conduct an honest self-assessment. God has not been mysterious about your design. The talents He has given you are the primary clues to the investments He wants you to make. Ask yourself:

- What are my spiritual gifts? (e.g., teaching, mercy, administration, hospitality, leadership). Are my primary commitments aligned with the way God has gifted me?

- What are my passions? What injustices in the world break my heart? What topics do I love to learn and talk about? These passions are often a signpost pointing toward your calling.

- What are my primary roles and responsibilities? For most of us, our core "yeses" are tied to the non-negotiable roles God has already placed us in: as a spouse, a parent, an employee, a church member. Faithfulness in these primary roles is the foundation of good stewardship. A "yes" to a new ministry that forces you to say "no" to your family is almost always a poor investment.

Third, seek wise counsel. Proverbs tells us that "without counsel plans fail, but with many advisers they succeed" (Proverbs 15:22). Find a few trusted, mature believers in your life and invite them to speak into this process. Ask them, "From your perspective, what do you see as my greatest strengths? Where do you see me being most fruitful? Where do you see me getting distracted or over-committed?" An outside perspective can often see our patterns more clearly than we can ourselves.

Through this process of prayer, self-assessment, and counsel, a clearer picture of your core "yeses" will begin to emerge. You can even write them down. You might end up with a personal mission statement or a short list of 3-5 core priorities for your current season. This list becomes your filter. When a new opportunity or request comes your way, you no longer have to make a decision based on fear or guilt. You can now hold it up to your list of divine priorities and ask a simple, objective question: "Does saying 'yes' to this help me advance my primary, God-given mission, or does it distract from it?" This is the tool that empowers a guilt-free, confident "no."

Conclusion: The Joy of a Focused Life

The life of a faithful steward is not a life of grim, joyless discipline. It is a life of profound peace and joyful effectiveness. The constant anxiety of a boundary-less existence is replaced by the calm confidence of a focused life. The frustration of being spread too thin is replaced by the satisfaction of doing a few things well.

When you say "no" to the things that are outside your calling, you create the margin to bring your best self to the things that are inside it. Your family gets a more present and energetic spouse and parent. Your church gets a more focused and effective servant. Your work gets a more creative and productive employee. And you get the deep, abiding joy of knowing that you are co-laboring with God, investing your one precious life in the things that have eternal significance.

This is the ultimate purpose of saying "no." It is not about deprivation; it is about delight. It is the discipline that allows us to say a wholehearted, unreserved, and joyful "yes" to God. It is the sacred mandate of a steward, faithfully managing the master's resources, and waiting with eager anticipation to hear those beautiful, life-affirming words: "Well done, good and faithful servant. You have been faithful over a little; I will set you over much. Enter into the joy of your master."

Reflection Questions:

1. Read the Parable of the Talents in Matthew 25:14-30. How does the master's condemnation of the "wicked and slothful" servant for playing it safe challenge your own ideas about faithfulness?

2. If you were to honestly assess your life right now, would you describe it as that of a wise investor or a careless spender of your time and energy? What is one specific area where you feel you are "squandering" your resources?

3. Take 15 minutes to do a quick inventory of your core roles and God-given passions. What are the 3-5 non-negotiable priorities that emerge from that list?

4. Think of a recent commitment you made. Did you evaluate it based on your divine priorities, or did you say "yes" based on fear, guilt, or impulse? How might having a written list of priorities have changed your decision?

A Prayer for Wise Stewardship

Generous God, I acknowledge that everything I have is a gift from You. My time, my talents, my very life—it is all a sacred trust. Forgive me for the times I have been a poor steward, squandering the precious resources You have given me. Teach me to number my days, that I might gain a heart of wisdom. Grant me the courage and discernment of a wise investor, to say "no" to lesser things so I can give my best "yes" to You. Holy Spirit, clarify my calling and my core priorities in this season. Help me to live a focused, fruitful, and joyful life, so that one day I may hear, "Well done." Amen.

Chapter Seven

Speaking the Truth in Love

We have arrived at the great turning point of our journey. The foundations have been laid, stone by heavy stone. We have established that boundaries are not only permissible but are a divine principle, woven into the very fabric of God's good creation. We have seen this principle modeled perfectly in the life of Christ, our ultimate example. We have confronted the internal enemies—the fear of man and the guilt complex—that keep us trapped in a cycle of compliance. We have embraced our high calling as wise stewards, understanding that a strategic "no" is the tool that unlocks a life of purposeful, God-honoring "yeses."

The "why" is now firmly in place. But for many of us, a daunting question remains: "How?" How, in the messy, complicated reality of our daily relationships, do we actually say the word? What does a godly, loving, and respectful "no" actually sound like? It is one thing to be convinced in the quiet of our study that we have the right to set a boundary; it is another thing entirely to find the right words when our pushy relative is on the phone, our demanding boss is standing over our desk, or a well-intentioned ministry leader is putting us on the spot.

This is where theory must become practice. And the Bible, in its profound wisdom, does not just give us the theology of boundaries; it gives us the communication strategy as well. The success or failure of a boundary often hinges not on the decision itself, but on its delivery. A necessary "no" delivered with harshness, anger, or defensiveness can inflict more damage than the boundary prevents. Conversely, a firm "no" delivered with grace, compassion, and respect can, paradoxically, strengthen a relationship even as it establishes a limit.

The guiding principle for this delicate art is found in the Apostle Paul's beautiful and challenging exhortation to the Ephesian church: "...speaking the truth in love, we are to grow up in every way into him who is the head, into Christ" (Ephesians 4:15). This single phrase, "speaking the truth in love," is the North Star for all Christ-honoring communication. It is the perfect balance, the divine equilibrium between the two extremes we so often fall into: either a brutal, loveless honesty that uses "truth" as a club, or a dishonest, truth-less "love" that prioritizes superficial harmony over authentic relationship. A godly boundary lives at the intersection of these two virtues. It is both absolutely true and absolutely loving.

The "Truth" Component: A Call to Clarity and Courage

Let's first examine the "truth" part of the equation. When it comes to setting boundaries, truth has several facets. First and foremost, it means being honest—honest with ourselves and honest with the other person. Many of us have become experts at the "soft yes," which is really a disguised "no." We say things like, "Let me think about it," "I'll see if I can make it work," or "That sounds interesting, I'll get back to you," when we know in our hearts that the answer is no. We do this to avoid the immediate discomfort of saying the word, but this dishonesty is a cruel kindness. It creates false hope for the other person and prolongs our own anxiety. The truthful approach is to be clear and direct from the outset.

Second, truth requires clarity. A vague or ambiguous boundary is no boundary at all. It invites negotiation and misunderstanding. Saying something like, "I'm just really busy right now," is not a clear boundary; it's a temporary excuse. The other person will likely come back next week when they assume you are less busy. A truthful, clear boundary sounds like, "Thank you for thinking of me for this project, but I am not able to take on any new commitments for the rest of this year." Or, "I appreciate the invitation, but I am reserving my Tuesday evenings for my family." The boundary is specific, leaving no room for misinterpretation.

It may feel more blunt in the moment, but it is ultimately much kinder because it is clear.

Finally, truth requires courage. As we've seen, setting a boundary often means pushing back against fear and guilt. Speaking the truth means you don't apologize for your limits, as if they are a personal failing. You don't over-explain and justify your "no" with a long list of reasons, which only communicates that your decision is up for debate. The truth is that you have a right to your limits, simply because they are your limits. Your time and energy are finite, and you are the steward of them. A simple, courageous, and truthful statement like, "I've prayerfully considered my commitments, and I'm not able to add that to my plate," is a complete answer. It is grounded in the truth of your stewardship, and it requires no further defense.

The "Love" Component: A Call to Compassion and Grace

If truth is the strong backbone of a godly boundary, then love is its warm and beating heart. Without love, our truthful "no" can become a cold, hard instrument of rejection. Paul reminds us that even if we have faith that can move mountains, if we have not love, we are nothing (1 Corinthians 13:2). The same is true for our boundaries.

What does love look like in the context of saying "no"? First, it means showing compassion and empathy. It is the ability to acknowledge the other person's need or desire, even as you decline to meet it. It communicates that you have heard them and that their request matters, even if your answer is no. This can be as simple as starting your response with an affirming phrase: "That sounds like a wonderful and important project..." or "I can hear how passionate you are about this, and I really respect that..." or "Thank you so much for trusting me enough to ask for my help with this..." This small act of validation softens the "no" that follows. It separates the rejection of the request from a rejection of the person.

Second, love is expressed through grace and kindness. This is where Colossians 4:6 provides a beautiful and practical image: "Let your speech always be gracious,

seasoned with salt, so that you may know how you ought to answer each person."
What does it mean for our words to be "seasoned with salt"? In the ancient world,
salt was a valuable commodity with several key properties. It was a preservative;
it stopped decay and kept things from going bad. A gracious, salt-seasoned "no"
seeks to preserve the relationship. Its goal is not to win an argument or to sever a
tie, but to set a limit in a way that allows the relationship to continue in a healthier
form.

Salt was also a flavoring agent; it made things palatable. A loving "no" is seasoned with words that make a difficult truth easier to swallow. This is about tone.
It's the difference between a flat, dismissive "No, I can't," and a warm, respectful,
"I wish I could help, but I'm not able to at this time." The message is the same,
but the flavor is entirely different.

Finally, salt was a symbol of purity. A loving "no" is pure in its motivation. It is
not passive-aggressive. It is not laced with resentment from all the times you said
"yes" when you wanted to say "no." It is not a power play designed to punish the
other person. It comes from a clean heart, a heart that is at peace with its decision
because it has been made prayerfully and with the goal of faithful stewardship.
The motivation is not selfish, but God-honoring.

The Heart of the Matter: Checking Your Motivation

This brings us to the most crucial element of speaking the truth in love: the
state of your own heart. Before you open your mouth to set a boundary, you
must perform a quick heart-check. What is your motivation? Are you setting
this boundary from a place of anger and resentment? Are you trying to punish
someone for their past demands? Is your "no" a passive-aggressive way of getting
back at them? If so, your words, no matter how carefully crafted, will likely be
tainted with the bitterness of your heart. As Jesus said, "out of the abundance of
the heart the mouth speaks" (Matthew 12:34).

A truly loving boundary comes from a heart that is at peace. It comes from a
place of quiet confidence in your identity in Christ and your calling as a stew-

ard. Your goal is not to control the other person's reaction. You cannot control whether they will be disappointed, angry, or understanding. Your goal is simply to be faithful in your communication—to speak the truth clearly, courageously, and with a genuine, compassionate, and loving spirit. You are responsible for the delivery; they are responsible for the reception.

Let's imagine a practical scenario. Your aging mother, who lives alone, has a pattern of calling you with non-urgent household tasks several times a week, often interrupting your work or your family time. You feel resentful and overwhelmed, but you've been saying "yes" out of guilt. Now, you've decided you need to set a boundary.

A boundary delivered from a heart of resentment might sound like this: "Mom, you have to stop calling me for every little thing! I have my own life, you know. I can't be your personal handyman 24/7." While the need for a boundary is true, the delivery is harsh, blaming, and loveless.

A boundary delivered from a heart of peace, speaking the truth in love, might sound like this: "Mom, I love you, and I want to be there to help you. I've been feeling a bit overwhelmed lately trying to balance work, my family, and being available for your needs. To make sure I can be fully present for the most important things, I'd like to set aside a specific time for us to handle these tasks. How about I come over every Saturday morning for a couple of hours? We can make a list during the week of anything you need, and I will be all yours during that time. For real emergencies, of course, you can call me anytime."

Do you see the difference? The truth is the same: "I cannot be on call for you 24/7." But the delivery is completely different. The second response is seasoned with salt. It affirms the love ("I love you"). It validates the relationship ("I want to be there to help you"). It speaks the truth honestly but gently, using "I" statements ("I've been feeling overwhelmed"). It offers a loving, proactive solution that honors both her need for help and your need for limits. This is the art of speaking the truth in love.

Conclusion: A Witness to a Watching World

Learning to say "no" with grace is more than just a life skill for avoiding burnout. It is a powerful form of Christian witness. Our world is starved for communication that is both truthful and loving. We are surrounded by a culture that often swings between the extremes of brutal, "tell-it-like-it-is" honesty that tears people down, and a superficial, conflict-avoidant "niceness" that is afraid to speak the truth.

When a Christian sets a boundary with courage, clarity, and genuine compassion, they are putting the character of Christ on display. They are showing the world that it is possible to be both strong and gentle, both principled and kind. They are demonstrating a relational wisdom that is deeply attractive and counter-cultural. Your gracious "no" can be one of the most compelling sermons you ever preach. It shows that your faith is not a recipe for becoming a doormat, but a path to becoming a person of deep integrity, profound love, and quiet strength—a person who, in every way, is growing up into the likeness of Christ.

Reflection Questions:

1. Think about a recent time you said "no" or avoided saying "no." On the spectrum between "brutal honesty" and "dishonest flattery," where did your communication fall? What is one thing you could have done differently to bring more truth or more love into the conversation?

2. The chapter describes a loving "no" as being "seasoned with salt." Using the metaphors of salt as a preservative, a flavoring, and a purifier, evaluate a boundary you need to set. How can you ensure your words will preserve the relationship, make the truth palatable, and come from a pure motive?

3. Practice rewriting a difficult "no" you need to deliver. Start by writing out the harsh, unfiltered version that reflects your frustration. Then, prayerfully rewrite it using the principles of speaking the truth in love

(affirming the person, using "I" statements, being clear, offering a loving alternative if appropriate).

4. What is the state of your heart concerning the person with whom you need to set a boundary? Do you need to spend time in prayer, confessing any resentment or anger, before you can have the conversation?

A Prayer for Gracious Speech

Lord, thank you for the gift of words. Forgive me for the times I have used them to wound with loveless truth, or to deceive with truth-less love. Fill my heart so full of Your love and Your truth that my speech would naturally reflect Your character. As I prepare to set the boundaries You have called me to, grant me the courage to be clear and the compassion to be kind. Let my words be gracious, seasoned with salt. Guard my heart from resentment and fear, so that I might speak from a place of peace and security in You. May my communication bring honor to Your name and be a witness to Your beautiful balance of truth and grace. Amen.

Chapter Eight

Scripts for Saying No

The principles are in place. Your heart is prepared. You understand the profound difference between a harsh rejection and a loving limit. You have committed to speaking the truth in love, seasoning your words with the salt of grace and compassion. Now, the moment of truth arrives. The phone rings, the email lands in your inbox, the person stands before you with an expectant look on their face, and a request is made. All the theology in the world can evaporate in the heat of that moment, leaving you fumbling for words, defaulting to old habits of compliance, and walking away with yet another unwanted commitment on your calendar.

This is the gap we aim to close in this chapter—the gap between intention and execution. If Chapter 7 was about the heart attitude of a godly "no," this chapter is about the practical language. We are moving from the workshop of the heart to the laboratory of our words. While there is no magic formula, no single phrase that will work in every situation, there are patterns, templates, and scripts that can equip us with the confidence to communicate our boundaries clearly, kindly, and effectively.

Think of this chapter as a language-learning guide. When you first learn a new language, you start by memorizing common phrases and practicing basic conversational scripts. It feels awkward and unnatural at first. You might stumble over the pronunciation or use a phrase in the wrong context. But with practice, those scripts become second nature. You begin to understand the underlying grammar, adapt the phrases to your own personality, and eventually, you can speak fluently and authentically.

So it is with the language of boundaries. The scripts that follow are your starter phrases. You may need to have them written on a notecard by your phone or practice them in front of a mirror. They may feel stiff or formal at first. But as you begin to use them, you will internalize the grammar of a healthy "no," and you will find your own authentic voice for speaking the truth in love.

The Anatomy of a Gracious "No"

Before we dive into specific scenarios, let's dissect a well-formed, gracious "no." Most effective boundary statements contain some combination of the following four elements. Not every situation will require all four, but understanding them gives you a versatile toolkit.

1. The Affirmation (The Bridge of Love): This is the opening statement that validates the person or the request. It's the spoonful of honey that helps the medicine go down. It communicates, "I hear you, and I value you," before you deliver the limit.

- Examples: "Thank you so much for thinking of me." "That sounds like a wonderful opportunity." "I really appreciate you trusting me enough to ask." "I can see how much this means to you."

2. The Clear Refusal (The Backbone of Truth): This is the core of the boundary. It must be simple, direct, and unambiguous. Avoid wishy-washy language that invites negotiation.

- Examples: "I'm not able to take that on." "My answer is no." "That's not going to be possible." "I'm going to have to decline."

3. The Brief, Honest Reason (The "Why" of Stewardship, Optional): This is not a defensive excuse, but a concise statement that links your "no" to your God-given priorities. It models wise stewardship and depersonalizes the refusal.

- Examples: "...because I'm committed to protecting my family evenings."

"...as that falls outside the scope of my current ministry focus." "...because I'm working to create more margin in my schedule for rest."

4. The Loving Alternative (The Open Door, Optional): When appropriate, you can offer a different, more bounded way to help, or empower the person to find another solution. This reinforces your goodwill and care.

- Examples: "I can't lead the committee, but I would be happy to spend 30 minutes brainstorming with the new leader." "I'm not able to commit on such short notice, but let's look at our calendars for sometime next month." "While I can't help you with that, have you considered reaching out to [another person or resource]?"

With these four components in our toolkit, let's apply them to some of the most common and challenging scenarios we face.

Scripts for Family Scenarios

Family relationships are often the most difficult place to begin setting boundaries because the history is long, the roles are deeply ingrained, and the emotional stakes are high.

Scenario 1: Saying no to a family member asking for money. Your brother, who has a history of poor financial decisions, calls to ask for a significant loan to cover his credit card debt. Your guilt flares, but you know that giving him the money will only enable his behavior.

- Less Effective (Guilt-driven, Vague): "Oh, wow. I don't know, man. Things are really tight for us right now. Let me talk to my spouse and see if we can move some things around. I'll call you back." (This is a "soft yes" that prolongs the anxiety and gives false hope).

- More Effective (Truth in Love): "(Affirmation) Brother, thank you for trusting me enough to come to me with this. I can hear how stressful this situation is for you. (Clear Refusal) After much prayer and discussion, my spouse and I have made a commitment not to lend money to family. So, our answer on the loan is no. (Brief Reason) We feel this is the best way for us to honor both our stewardship and our relationships. (Loving Alternative) However, we love you, and we are absolutely committed to helping you win with your finances. I would be thrilled to help you find a good financial coach, or to sit down with you and help you create a budget myself. We are on your team."

Scenario 2: Setting a boundary on unsolicited advice. Your well-meaning mother constantly offers unsolicited advice on how you should be raising your children, and it's beginning to cause friction.

- Less Effective (Passive-Aggressive): You listen silently on the phone, saying "uh-huh" while fuming on the inside, and then complain about her to your spouse later. (This avoids conflict but builds resentment).

- More Effective (Truth in Love): Choose a calm, non-confrontational moment. "Mom, (Affirmation) I know how much you love the kids, and I am so grateful for your wisdom and the role you play in their lives. (Clear Refusal/Boundary) Lately, though, I've been feeling a bit overwhelmed and insecure with all the parenting advice I've been getting. It would really help me if, moving forward, you could wait for me to ask for your advice before offering it. (Brief Reason) My spouse and I are really trying to find our own footing as parents, and we need the space to do that, even if we make some mistakes. (Affirmation) Please know that we do want your input, and we will definitely come to you when we're feeling stuck. We love you."

Scripts for Workplace Scenarios

Workplace boundaries are crucial for preventing burnout and maintaining a healthy work-life balance, but they can be intimidating due to power dynamics.

Scenario 3: Declining a project outside of your work hours. Your boss emails you at 7 PM, asking you to complete a non-urgent report by the next morning.

- Less Effective (People-Pleasing): You immediately respond, "Yes, of course!" and then stay up late, sacrificing sleep and family time, feeling resentful.

- More Effective (Professional, Truth in Love): Wait to respond until the next morning during work hours. "(Affirmation) Thanks for sending this over. I can see that getting this report done is a priority. (Clear Refusal/Boundary) As a rule, I keep my evenings reserved for my family, so I am just seeing this now. (Loving Alternative) I can shift my priorities this morning and I will have it on your desk by noon. In the future, for non-emergency tasks, a 24-hour heads-up would be a great help for me to plan my workload effectively."

Scripts for Church and Ministry Scenarios

The church should be the safest place to have healthy boundaries, but often the fear of being seen as "unspiritual" makes it the hardest.

Scenario 4: Being asked to join another committee. You are already serving faithfully in one ministry, and the chairperson of the nominating committee approaches you in the church hallway to lead a new initiative.

- Less Effective (On-the-Spot, Vague): "Oh! Wow. That's an honor. Uh, sure, I guess I could probably make that work." (You've just committed out of pressure, without prayerful consideration).

- More Effective (Buys Time, Honors Stewardship): "(Affirmation) Wow, thank you so much for considering me for that role. I'm honored. (Clear Boundary on the Decision-Making Process) I have a personal policy of never saying 'yes' to a new ministry commitment on the spot. I need to take a few days to pray about it and discuss it with my family to see if it aligns with what God has called me to in this season. (Clear Next Step) Can I get back to you by Friday?"

- Follow-up (If the answer is no): "(Affirmation) After praying about it, I have such a sense of peace that God is calling me to remain focused on my current ministry with the youth. (Clear Refusal) So, I have to decline the invitation to lead the new initiative. (Loving Alternative) I will be praying for you as you seek out the right person for that role. I know God has someone prepared for it."

Scripts for Friendship Scenarios

Healthy friendships are built on mutual respect, which includes respecting each other's limits.

Scenario 5: Saying no to a social event. A group of friends invites you to a late-night concert on a weeknight, but you know you need your sleep to be effective at work and with your family the next day.

- Less Effective (Makes up an Excuse): "Oh, I can't, I think I have a dentist appointment that day." (This is a lie that can easily be found out, and it communicates that you need an "excuse" to say no).

- More Effective (Honest, Loving): "(Affirmation) That sounds like so much fun! I'm bummed I'll have to miss it. (Clear Refusal) I'm going to have to pass on this one. (Brief, Honest Reason) I've learned the hard way that I'm a wreck if I don't get enough sleep on a work night. (Loving Alternative) But please send me pictures, and let's definitely plan to get together on the weekend soon!"

The Power of the Simple "No" and the Strategic Pause

While the four-part structure is a great tool, not every situation requires it. Sometimes, particularly when dealing with a manipulative person, a high-pressure salesperson, or a repeated boundary-pusher, the most loving and truthful response is a simple, polite, and firm "no."

- "No, thank you."

- "No, I'm not interested."

- "No."

You do not owe anyone a lengthy explanation. A simple "no" is a complete sentence. Do not let anyone bully you into justifying your limits.

Furthermore, one of the most powerful tools in your new toolkit is the strategic pause. As we saw in the church scenario, you are rarely required to give an immediate answer. You can almost always buy yourself time to think, pray, and consult your priorities. Memorize these phrases:

- "Let me check my calendar and my list of priorities, and I will get back to you."

- "I need to think and pray about that before I can give you an answer."

- "My policy is not to give an immediate answer to new requests. I'll let you know by tomorrow."

This pause is your best defense against the pressure of an on-the-spot demand. It allows you to move from a reactive decision based on fear or guilt to a proactive decision based on your calling as a steward.

Conclusion: Practice Makes Proficient

Learning this new language will take time. You will make mistakes. You will have moments where you revert to your old patterns. That's okay. Give yourself grace. The goal is not perfection; it is faithful progress. Start with one low-stakes scenario this week. Choose one of these scripts and adapt it to your own voice. Practice it. Use it. Then, notice what happens. You will likely discover that the catastrophic reaction you feared never materializes. You will feel a sense of peace and integrity. You will feel the strength of a city whose walls are being rebuilt, stone by stone.

With each small act of courageous communication, you are not just managing your schedule; you are retraining your soul. You are teaching yourself, and those around you, that you are a person of purpose, a wise steward, and a follower of the One who spoke the truth with perfect, life-giving love.

Reflection Questions:

1. Of the four components of a gracious "no" (Affirmation, Clear Refusal, Brief Reason, Loving Alternative), which one do you find easiest to do? Which one is the most challenging for you, and why?

2. Choose one of the scenarios in this chapter that feels most relevant to your life right now. Take the "More Effective" script and rewrite it in your own words, so it sounds authentic to you. Practice saying it out loud.

3. Identify a low-stakes opportunity in the coming week where you can practice a simple "no" or a strategic pause. What is the situation, and what will you say?

4. How does the idea of these scripts being like a "new language" give you grace for the learning process? What is one thing you can do to encourage yourself when you feel awkward or make a mistake?

A Prayer for Courageous Words

Lord, You are the Word made flesh, the perfect communicator of truth and love. I ask that You would guide my words. Give me the wisdom to know what to say and the courage to say it. As I learn this new language of healthy boundaries, please bring these principles and scripts to my mind in the moments I need them most. Help me to be patient with myself in the process. Replace my fear of awkwardness with a desire for faithfulness. May the words of my mouth and the meditation of my heart be pleasing to you, O LORD, my rock and my redeemer. Amen.

Chapter Nine

When Your "No" Isn't Respected

You have done the hard and holy work. You have prepared your heart, clarified your priorities, and chosen your words with prayerful care. You have taken a deep breath and, speaking the truth in love, you have delivered your gracious "no." You have set your boundary. In a perfect world, the other person would say, "Thank you for your honesty. I understand and respect your limits." And sometimes, in healthy and mature relationships, that is exactly what happens. But as we know all too well, we do not live in a perfect world.

More often than not, especially when you are trying to change a long-standing relational dynamic, your newfound "no" will be met not with acceptance, but with resistance. This resistance is the critical test of your resolve. It is the moment the storm hits the new wall you have built. If the wall holds, the foundation of a new, healthier relationship is laid. If it crumbles under the first wave of pressure, the old, unhealthy patterns will rush back in with even greater force, and it will be that much harder to rebuild in the future.

This chapter is about what to do when the storm hits. It is about how to stand firm when your "no" isn't respected. This is not the time for complex new strategies. It is the time for calm, courageous consistency. It is about understanding the tactics of pushback, grounding yourself in the truth, and learning to hold your boundary with a gentle strength that is neither aggressive nor passive. This is where the true, character-forging work of a bounded life begins.

The Predictable Pushback: Why Resistance is Normal

Before we diagnose the specific tactics of resistance, it is crucial to understand why it happens. Pushback is not necessarily a sign that you have set your boundary incorrectly. In fact, it is often a sign that you have set a necessary one. Resistance is a normal and predictable part of changing any system, and a family or a friendship is a relational system.

For years, you may have played a specific role in that system: the compliant one, the rescuer, the peacekeeper, the ever-available one. The other people in the system grew accustomed to that role. They built their own patterns of behavior around your predictability. When you suddenly change the rules by saying "no," you are disrupting the entire system. Their resistance is an attempt to pull you back into your old role and restore the system to its familiar, albeit unhealthy, equilibrium. They are not necessarily being malicious (though sometimes they are); they are simply reacting to a change they did not ask for and do not like. Understanding this can help you depersonalize the pushback. It's not just about you; it's about the disruption of a long-standing, predictable dance.

Common Tactics of Resistance

When someone wants to challenge your boundary, they will often resort to a predictable set of tactics. Recognizing these tactics is the first step to disarming them.

1. Guilt-Tripping and Manipulation: This is the most common tactic, especially in close relationships. It involves statements designed to make you feel selfish, unloving, or unspiritual for setting a limit.

- Examples: "I guess I just can't count on you anymore." "A good Christian would have a more servant-hearted attitude." "After all I've done for you, this is how you repay me?" "I guess your new friends are more important than your family now."

2. Anger and Intimidation: When guilt doesn't work, some people will escalate to anger. This is an attempt to bully you into submission. The goal is to make the consequence of holding your boundary (their anger) more frightening than the consequence of giving in.

- Examples: Raising their voice, using harsh or critical language, making threats ("If you don't do this, don't bother calling me again"), or giving you the silent treatment.

3. Questioning and Debating: This tactic seeks to undermine your boundary by treating it as an opinion that is up for debate. The person will pick apart your reasons, challenge your logic, and try to draw you into an argument, hoping to wear you down until you concede.

- Examples: "Why can't you? Just give me one good reason." "That doesn't make any sense. You helped so-and-so with the exact same thing last month." "Are you sure you've really thought this through?"

4. Playing the Victim: This is a subtle form of manipulation where the person frames your boundary as a direct and painful attack on them. Their goal is to make you feel like a cruel aggressor, forcing you to retract your boundary to prove you are a kind person.

- Examples: "I can't believe you're hurting me like this." "Everyone always abandons me." "Fine, I'll just sit here and suffer alone."

When you are on the receiving end of these tactics, your natural, fleshly response will be to fight (get angry and defensive), flee (give in immediately), or freeze (get flustered and say nothing). The spiritual path, however, is a fourth way: the way of calm, consistent, gentle strength.

The Biblical Response: A Gentle Answer and a Firm Resolve

The book of Proverbs gives us our core strategy: "A gentle answer turns away wrath, but a harsh word stirs up anger" (Proverbs 15:1). Your first and best response to pushback is not to match its emotional intensity, but to meet it with a surprising and disarming gentleness. This does not mean you are backing down. It means you are refusing to get drawn into the emotional chaos. You are maintaining your internal peace and responding from a place of strength, not reactivity.

Your goal is to be a broken record. You simply repeat the boundary, often in the exact same words, with the same calm and respectful tone. You do not need to invent new defenses; you simply need to restate your decision.

Let's apply this to our tactics:

- When they guilt-trip: "(Gentle Answer) I can hear that you are disappointed. (Repeat the Boundary) And, my answer is still no."

- When they get angry: "(Gentle Answer) I'm not going to argue with you, but my decision is final." Or, if the anger is escalating, "I can see that you are very upset. I am going to end this conversation for now. We can talk again when we are both calmer."

- When they try to debate: "(Gentle Answer) I've already made my decision, and I'm not going to debate it with you." You must refuse to JADE: Justify, Argue, Defend, or Explain. The moment you start defending your "no," you have given them power and communicated that your boundary is negotiable.

- When they play the victim: "(Gentle Answer) It is never my intention to hurt you. (Repeat the Boundary) However, this is a boundary I need to have for my own well-being, and I am going to stick with it."

In every case, you are holding two things in tension: you are being soft on the person but hard on the issue. Your tone is gentle, affirming, and respectful of them as a person. But your resolve on the boundary itself is firm, clear, and unyielding.

This combination is profoundly powerful. It refuses to escalate the conflict while also refusing to surrender the boundary.

When to Create Distance: The Boundary of Last Resort

What happens when the pushback is relentless? What about a person who, week after week, continues to rage, manipulate, or disrespect your limits? The Bible is clear that while we are to be patient and gentle, we are not called to endlessly subject ourselves to toxic or abusive behavior. There comes a point where the most loving thing you can do—for yourself and for the other person—is to create distance.

Proverbs repeatedly warns us not to engage with a "fool" or a "scoffer"—that is, someone who is not open to reason and who consistently responds with contempt. "Do not speak in the hearing of a fool, for he will despise the wisdom of your words" (Proverbs 23:9). Paul is even more direct in his letter to Titus: "As for a person who stirs up division, after warning him once and then twice, have nothing more to do with him" (Titus 3:10).

Setting a boundary of distance is a last resort, but it is a necessary one in cases of emotional, verbal, or physical abuse, or with individuals who have proven over time that they will not honor any of your internal or verbal boundaries. This may look like limiting your contact with them, only interacting with them in public places, or in severe cases, choosing to end the relationship for a season or permanently for the sake of your own safety and sanity. This is not an act of unforgiveness or hatred. It is an act of profound stewardship of your own life, recognizing that you cannot be a healthy, fruitful person for God if you are constantly being torn down by a toxic relationship.

Conclusion: The Test That Forges Your Freedom

The period of resistance after you set a new boundary is one of the most significant tests of your spiritual journey. It is the moment where everything you have learned in this book is put into practice. It is the crucible where your resolve is forged. Every time you hold firm to a boundary with gentle strength, you are doing several things at once.

You are teaching others how to treat you. You are communicating that your limits are real and that you respect yourself enough to enforce them. You are also strengthening your own "courage muscle," making it easier to hold firm the next time. Most importantly, you are declaring where your ultimate trust lies. You are choosing to weather the storm of another person's disapproval because you are anchored in the safety of God's unconditional approval.

The pushback will not last forever. As you consistently hold your new boundaries, a new normal will begin to emerge. The people who truly love and respect you will eventually adapt. They will learn to honor your limits, and your relationship will be rebuilt on a new and healthier foundation of honesty and mutual respect. And for those who refuse to adapt, their continued resistance will be a clear sign that a greater distance may be the wisest and most loving path forward.

Do not be discouraged by the storm. It is a sign that the walls are going up. Stand firm, stay gentle, and trust that the God who commanded the chaotic sea to respect its boundaries is the same God who will give you the strength to maintain yours.

Reflection Questions:

1. Think about a relationship where you are afraid to set a boundary. Which of the "Common Tactics of Resistance" do you most anticipate receiving?

2. The chapter emphasizes being "soft on the person but hard on the issue." What does this look like practically in a difficult relationship in your life? How can you show love and respect for the person while still holding firm to your limit?

3. The acronym JADE (Justify, Argue, Defend, Explain) is a tool to stop you from getting drawn into a debate. In which of your relationships

are you most tempted to JADE when you set a boundary? What could you say instead?

4. Have you ever had to set a boundary of distance with someone? If so, what led to that decision? If not, how does the idea that this can be a loving, biblical last resort make you feel?

A Prayer for Gentle Strength

Lord, my Rock and my Fortress, I know that setting new boundaries will be a test. When the pushback comes, I pray for your strength to stand firm. Fill me with your Holy Spirit, that I might not respond with fear or anger, but with a supernatural, gentle strength. Give me a gentle answer that can turn away wrath. Help me to be a broken record, calmly and kindly repeating the truth. Lord, protect my heart from manipulation and intimidation. Remind me in the heat of the moment that my security is in You alone. Give me the wisdom to know when to persevere and when to create distance. May I honor You in all things, a faithful steward of my life and my relationships. Amen.

Chapter Ten

From People-Pleaser to God-Pleaser

The journey we have been on is not for the faint of heart. To stand against the tide of expectations, to face the pushback of those we love, to wrestle with the deep-seated fear and guilt within our own souls—this is the difficult and holy work of discipleship. It can feel, in the moment, like a battle for survival, a series of tense conversations and awkward moments that leave us feeling drained and uncertain. If our focus remains only on the struggle, we can easily become discouraged. We might be tempted to ask, "Is all this effort really worth it?"

This chapter is the resounding, hope-filled "Yes!" It is the view from the top of the mountain after a long and arduous climb. It is the first taste of the sweet fruit after a season of difficult tilling and planting. The work of setting boundaries is not an end in itself. The goal is not simply to become proficient at saying "no." The goal is the harvest. The difficult, temporary season of establishing and defending your limits is the necessary groundwork for a lifetime of flourishing in a way you may have never thought possible.

This is the great exchange offered to us in the gospel. We trade the heavy, ill-fitting yoke of people-pleasing for the light and easy yoke of Christ. We trade the chains of obligation for the glorious freedom of the children of God. The entire process is a profound transformation of our identity, a slow and steady migration of the soul from one country to another. We are moving from the land of the People-Pleaser, a land governed by fear and anxiety, to the land of the God-Pleaser, a land governed by love, peace, and purpose. And the fruit that grows in this new land is sweeter than anything we could have imagined.

The Great Exchange: Trading Your Chains for Freedom

Jesus made a staggering promise to his followers: "So if the Son sets you free, you will be free indeed" (John 8:36). For many Christians, this freedom feels like an abstract theological concept, a future hope rather than a present reality. We believe we are saved, yet we live our daily lives in bondage—to the opinions of others, to the weight of false guilt, to the tyranny of our own over-committed schedules. The practice of setting biblical boundaries is one of the primary ways we begin to walk in the reality of the freedom Christ has already purchased for us. It is the act of taking hold of our spiritual birthright.

This freedom is not a vague, ethereal feeling; it is a concrete, multi-faceted reality that transforms every area of our lives. First and foremost, we experience freedom from the bondage of expectations. The life of a people-pleaser is the life of a slave, constantly trying to anticipate and meet the endless demands of a thousand different masters. It is a life of performance, of wearing masks, of carefully curating an image of being the "nice," "helpful," or "committed" one. This is an exhausting and joyless existence.

When you begin to root your identity in the unshakable truth of God's love for you, the expectations of others lose their power. You are liberated from the frantic dance of managing everyone's perceptions. You realize that your worth is not up for a vote. It was established by a divine decree and sealed with the blood of Christ. This freedom is palpable. It is the deep breath you take when you realize you don't have to perform anymore. You can be honest. You can have limits. You can be human. You are free to be the person God actually created you to be, not the person everyone else expects you to be.

Second, we experience freedom from the weight of false guilt. As we saw in Chapter 5, the guilt complex is a heavy backpack filled with responsibilities that were never ours to carry. We walk through life stooped over, weighed down by the burden of fixing everyone, rescuing everyone, and making everyone happy. When we embrace the biblical distinction between burdens and loads, we are given divine permission to set that backpack down.

The relief is immediate and profound. It is the freedom of a clear conscience, of knowing that you are responsible to God for your own faithfulness, not for the outcomes of everyone else's life. You are free to love people without the toxic pressure of needing to control them. You can offer help from a place of genuine compassion, not from a place of anxious obligation. You can sleep at night, trusting that God is sovereign and that He is at work in the lives of your loved ones in ways that are far beyond your capacity to manage.

Finally, we experience freedom from the tyranny of the urgent. The boundary-less life is a reactive life. Your schedule is a pinball machine, with every new email, text message, and "urgent" request sending you careening in a different direction. There is no time for deep work, for quiet reflection, for proactive planning. You are simply moving from one fire to the next, perpetually behind, perpetually stressed.

A bounded life is a proactive life. By saying "no" to the tyranny of the urgent, you create the margin to say "yes" to the truly important. You are no longer a slave to your inbox; you are a steward of your calling. This freedom allows you to think, to dream, to pray, to plan. It is the freedom to invest your best energy in your highest priorities, to live a life of intention and purpose, guided by the gentle whisper of the Holy Spirit rather than the loud shouting of the crowd.

The Garden of the Soul: How Boundaries Cultivate the Fruit of the Spirit

This newfound freedom is not an empty space; it is a fertile garden. The very act of setting boundaries creates the conditions necessary for the fruit of the Spirit, described in Galatians 5:22-23, to grow and ripen in our lives. A boundary-less life is like trying to grow a garden in the middle of a busy highway. The soil is constantly being trampled, the seeds can never take root, and any small sprout is quickly crushed. Boundaries are the fence we build around the garden of our soul, protecting it so that the Holy Spirit can do His beautiful work within us.

Consider how a bounded life cultivates this fruit. The first, and greatest, is love. We might think that saying "no" is unloving, but the opposite is true. The "yes" of a people-pleaser is often tainted with resentment, fear, and obligation. It is a love rooted in compulsion, not compassion. But when you are free to say "no," your "yes" becomes a pure and precious gift. It is offered freely, joyfully, and with a whole heart. You are now able to love people authentically, for who they are, not for the approval they can give you. This is the genuine, agape love that the Spirit desires to produce in us.

Next, consider joy and peace. The life of a people-pleaser is fundamentally joyless and chaotic. It is filled with the anxiety of performance and the internal turmoil of a life out of alignment with one's true convictions. When you begin to live a life of integrity, where your actions align with your God-given priorities, a deep and abiding peace settles into your soul. The internal war is over. The joy that follows is not the fleeting happiness of receiving someone's approval, but the solid, unshakeable joy of pleasing the Lord. It is the joy of a steward who knows they are being faithful to their Master's call.

A bounded life also cultivates patience, kindness, and goodness. It is nearly impossible to be patient when you are stretched to your breaking point. It is difficult to be genuinely kind when you are operating from an empty well of emotional energy. When you are constantly overwhelmed, your responses are more likely to be curt, irritable, and resentful. But when you have created margin in your life through healthy boundaries, you have the emotional and spiritual reserves to be patient with a struggling child, to show kindness to a difficult coworker, and to do good for your neighbor, not out of duty, but out of a genuine overflow of the heart.

Finally, consider faithfulness, gentleness, and self-control. Faithfulness, as we saw in the chapter on stewardship, is about being true to our primary calling. Boundaries are the tool that allows us to be faithful to the few things God has given us, rather than unfaithful in many. Gentleness, as we saw in the last chapter, is the spirit in which we hold our boundaries. It is a strength under control, a confidence so rooted in God's love that it has no need for harshness or aggression. And self-control is both the engine and the fruit of the entire process. The act of self-control required to set a boundary produces a life that is characterized by ever-increasing self-control. It is the beautiful, self-perpetuating cycle of a Spirit-filled life.

A New Identity: Living for an Audience of One

Ultimately, the harvest of a healthy "no" is a new identity. The entire journey is a process of dethroning the thousands of tiny tyrants we have allowed to rule our lives—the opinions of our friends, the expectations of our family, the demands of our culture—and enthroning the one true and loving King. It is the process of learning to live for an Audience of One.

When you live for an Audience of One, you are set free from the exhausting burden of the stage. You no longer have to perform, to manage your image, to adjust your mask for every new person you meet. You can simply be. You can rest in the finished work of Christ and the unconditional love of your Father. His is the only opinion that truly matters. His smile is the only applause you truly need. His "Well done" is the only review that has eternal significance.

This is not a self-centered life, but a God-centered one. And paradoxically, it is from this God-centered place that we are finally free to love other people well. We are no longer using them to meet our need for approval. We are no longer serving them out of a desperate attempt to secure our own worth. We can now love them for their sake. We can serve them from a place of fullness, not emptiness. We can offer our time, our resources, and our hearts as a free gift, with no strings attached, because we already have everything we need in Christ.

Conclusion: The Joyful Harvest

The path to a bounded life often begins with a painful "no." It is a "no" to old patterns, a "no" to familiar roles, a "no" to the demands that have defined us for years. It can feel like a loss, a death to our old way of being. And in many ways, it is. But as Jesus taught us, "unless a grain of wheat falls into the earth and dies, it remains alone; but if it dies, it bears much fruit" (John 12:24).

The initial, difficult death of our people-pleasing self is the necessary planting for a glorious harvest. The fruit of that harvest is a life of freedom you never thought possible. It is a life of deep and abiding peace, even in the midst of storms. It is a life of authentic, resilient joy, rooted not in circumstances, but in the pleasure of your Father. It is a life of purpose, where your finite and precious energy is invested in the things that will last for eternity.

This is not a distant, unattainable ideal. This is your birthright as a child of God. This is the abundant life that Jesus came to give you. Embrace the difficult work of setting boundaries, and trust that the one who began this good work in you will carry it on to completion, until your life becomes a beautiful, flourishing garden, bearing much fruit for His glory.

Reflection Questions:

1. In which area of your life do you most long to experience the freedom Christ promises (freedom from expectations, from guilt, or from the urgent)? What is one boundary that might be a first step toward that freedom?

2. Of the nine fruits of the Spirit listed in Galatians 5, which one feels most absent from your life right now due to a lack of boundaries? How do you see a healthy "no" creating the space for that fruit to grow?

3. What does it mean for you, practically, to live for an "Audience of One"? What is one decision you might make differently this week if God's approval was the only approval you were seeking?

4. The chapter describes the initial discomfort of setting boundaries as a seed "dying" in order to bear fruit. What old, people-pleasing pattern in your life do you need to let "die" so that a new harvest can grow?

A Prayer for a Fruitful Life

Father, thank you for the promise of freedom in your Son, Jesus. I confess that I have often lived as a slave to the expectations of others, and I have missed out on the fullness of the life you have for me. I ask that you would help me to walk in the freedom you have purchased. Uproot the people-pleasing patterns in my heart and replace them with a singular desire to please You. Lord, I want my life to be a garden that bears the fruit of your Spirit. Help me to build the protective fences of healthy boundaries, so that love, joy, peace, and all the other fruits may grow in me for your glory. Make me a faithful steward, a joyful servant, and a courageous follower of Christ, in whose name I pray. Amen.

Chapter Eleven

Earning True Respect

One of the most powerful snares that keeps us trapped in a people-pleasing lifestyle is the fear of losing respect. We believe, on a deep and visceral level, that our value in our community—our family, our workplace, our church—is directly proportional to our availability and our agreeableness. We think that to be respected, we must be the one who always says "yes," who always has time, who never disappoints. The word "no" feels like a direct withdrawal from our relational bank account, an act that will surely diminish our standing in the eyes of others. So we say "yes" to preserve our reputation, to be seen as the dependable, servant-hearted, team player.

But this is a profound and tragic misunderstanding of what it means to be respected. The path of the people-pleaser does not, in the end, lead to respect. It leads to being taken for granted. It leads to being seen as a useful resource, a convenient utility, but not necessarily as a person of substance and integrity. The person who is always available is, ironically, often the person whose time is valued the least.

This chapter is about turning our understanding of respect on its head. The surprising, paradoxical truth is this: healthy boundaries are the very foundation upon which genuine, lasting respect is built. While the initial act of setting a boundary may cause temporary disappointment or friction, the long-term result is a deeper, more authentic form of honor. People may not always like your boundaries, but they will, in time, respect the person who has the courage to set them. We will discover that the respect we so desperately crave is not found by erasing our limits, but by defining them with grace and conviction.

The Foundation: From Self-Respect to Mutual Respect

The journey to earning respect from others begins with the non-negotiable first step of respecting yourself. You cannot expect anyone else to value your time, your energy, or your priorities if you do not demonstrate that you value them first. Every time you allow your schedule to be hijacked, every time you say "yes" when your body is screaming for rest, every time you sacrifice a core priority for a lesser demand, you are sending a clear message to yourself and to the world: "My needs don't matter. My limits are not important. My calling can wait."

Setting a boundary is, at its core, an act of profound self-respect. It is the declaration that you are a steward, not a slave. It is the quiet, confident assertion that the life God has given you is a precious gift, worthy of being protected and cultivated. When you say, "I'm sorry, I'm not available on Thursday evenings, as that is my protected family time," you are not just declining a request; you are honoring the sacredness of your role as a spouse or parent. When you say, "I need to get back to you after I've had time to pray about that," you are honoring your relationship with God as the ultimate source of your guidance.

This act of self-respect is the foundation upon which all other respect is built. People learn how to treat us by observing how we treat ourselves. When they see that you are a person who takes your own commitments seriously, who values your own well-being, and who operates from a clear set of principles, they will naturally begin to treat you with a higher degree of consideration. They may not even be conscious of the shift, but they will begin to approach you with more respect for your time and your opinion, because you have modeled it for them.

The Framework of Trust: How Boundaries Create Reliability

Respect is inextricably linked to trust. We respect people we can rely on, people whose character is consistent and whose word is their bond. This is where the boundary-less person, despite their best intentions, ultimately fails. Their "yes," because it is given so freely and often under pressure, is an unreliable currency. They over-commit and under-deliver. They show up late and exhausted. They agree to things and then back out at the last minute. Their desire to please everyone results in them disappointing everyone, including themselves.

A person with healthy boundaries, on the other hand, becomes a pillar of reliability. Because they say "no" to the things outside their capacity and calling, their "yes" becomes a solid and trustworthy commitment. When they say, "Yes, I will be there," you can count on it. When they say, "Yes, I will have that done by Friday," the task gets done. They are not pulled in a thousand directions, so they can give their focused, wholehearted attention to the commitments they do make. As Jesus taught, "Let your 'yes' be yes, and your 'no,' no" (Matthew 5:37). A person with boundaries lives out this principle. Their words have weight and integrity.

This is precisely the kind of character that the Bible calls us to cultivate as a witness to the world. Paul's instruction to the young pastor Timothy is a masterclass in earning respect through character: "Let no one despise you for your youth, but set the believers an example in speech, in conduct, in love, in faith, in purity" (1 Timothy 4:12). Respect is not earned by being compliant; it is earned by being an example. A person who manages their life with the wisdom of healthy boundaries is a living example of self-control, faithfulness, and integrity.

Similarly, Paul tells Titus that a leader should exhibit "sound speech that cannot be condemned, so that an opponent may be put to shame, having nothing evil to say about us" (Titus 2:8). A life of well-kept boundaries is a life that cannot be easily condemned. Your opponent may not like your decisions, but they cannot accuse you of being unreliable, chaotic, or a hypocrite. Your conduct is consistent.

Your life has a certain weight, a gravitas, that silences critics and earns the respect of even those who might disagree with you.

The Kindness of Clarity: Why an Honest "No" is Better Than a Resentful "Yes"

One of the greatest lies of people-pleasing is that it is always kinder to say "yes." We think we are sparing someone's feelings by agreeing to something we don't have the time or desire to do. But a resentful "yes" is a relational poison. It is a seed of bitterness that we plant in our own hearts, and its toxic fruit will inevitably show up in our attitude and our actions.

When you say "yes" but mean "no," you are not truly serving the other person. You are serving them with a grudge. Your work will be half-hearted. Your attitude will be strained. You will communicate your displeasure through passive-aggressive sighs, subtle complaints, or a general lack of warmth. The other person, though they may not be able to name it, will feel the coldness of your obligation. They will sense that they are a burden to you. Is this truly a kinder or more loving outcome than an honest, gracious "no" at the outset?

An honest "no" is an act of profound respect for the other person. It respects them enough to tell them the truth. It respects their time and their goals by allowing them to find someone who can help with a whole and willing heart. Imagine you are organizing a major event and you ask someone to take on a key role. Which would you prefer? A person who says, "Yes," and then does a mediocre job while complaining under their breath? Or a person who says, "Thank you for asking. I've looked at my commitments, and I know I can't give that role the attention it deserves. My answer is no, but I will be cheering you on and praying for you to find the perfect person"? The second response, while initially disappointing, is infinitely more helpful and respectful. It is the response of a person you can trust.

Conclusion: The Weight of a Principled Life

In the end, the respect we all long for is not the fleeting popularity that comes from being agreeable. It is the deep, abiding honor that is given to a person of principle and integrity. It is the respect that is earned by a life well-lived, a life that has substance and weight. And that weight comes from having a strong, internal core of God-given purpose, protected by the courageous and consistent application of healthy boundaries.

When you become a person who is governed by a clear set of priorities, whose "yes" is trustworthy and whose "no" is gracious, you become a source of stability in a chaotic world. You become a safe person. People know what to expect from you. They know that your actions are not dictated by the shifting winds of popular opinion or emotional pressure, but by a steady and prayerful commitment to your calling.

This is the kind of person who is sought out for wise counsel. This is the kind of person who is entrusted with great responsibility. This is the kind of person who, like the noble woman described in Proverbs 31, is "clothed with strength and dignity" and can "laugh at the days to come." She is not anxious or frantic, because her life is in order. The result? "Her children rise up and call her blessed; her husband also, and he praises her." She has earned the deepest respect from those who know her best.

This is the harvest that awaits you on the other side of the difficult work of setting boundaries. You will trade the shallow, exhausting pursuit of being liked for the deep, soul-satisfying reality of being respected. You will become a person of substance, a pillar of trust, and a powerful example of a life lived with courage, conviction, and Christ-like integrity.

Reflection Questions:

1. Think of someone in your life whom you deeply respect. What specific qualities in them earn your respect? How many of those qualities are related to their consistency, integrity, and the way they manage their

commitments?

2. In what specific area of your life do you feel you are treated more like a "useful resource" than a respected person? How might setting one clear boundary begin to change that dynamic?

3. Recall a time you gave a resentful "yes." How did it affect your attitude and the quality of your work? How did it impact your relationship with the person you were "helping"?

4. First Timothy 4:12 calls us to be an "example." How does living a well-bounded life set an example for others in your family, workplace, or church? What message does it send to a watching world?

A Prayer for a Respectable Life

Father, I confess that I have often sought the approval of people more than I have sought to live a life worthy of respect. I have traded integrity for agreeableness and conviction for compliance. Forgive me. Lord, I ask that you would build in me the character of Christ. Clothe me with strength and dignity. Make me a person whose speech and conduct are an example to others. Give me the courage to set the boundaries that will make my "yes" a trustworthy promise. Help me to live with such integrity that even my opponents can find nothing evil to say about me. May my life not be light and chaotic, but have the weight and substance that comes from being firmly anchored in You. Make me a person worthy of respect, not for my own glory, but for the honor of Your holy name. Amen.

Chapter Twelve

Creating Deeper, More Authentic Relationships

We have come to the end of the path, to the final and perhaps most important harvest of a well-bounded life. And it is here that we must confront the deepest fear that fuels our people-pleasing. It is a fear that predates all others, a primal anxiety that sits at the very core of our being: the fear of being alone. We are created for connection. From the moment God declared, "It is not good for the man to be alone," relationship has been woven into the very fabric of our design. And so, we reason, if relationship is the goal, then anything that seems to threaten it must be wrong. Saying "no" feels like a threat. It feels like pushing people away, like building walls, like choosing isolation over connection. We play out the scenario in our minds: if I start setting limits, my friends will stop calling, my family will feel rejected, my church will see me as uncommitted, and I will end up disconnected and alone.

If this fear has been a quiet companion throughout your reading of this book, it is time to face it directly. Because the truth, in one of the most beautiful paradoxes of the Christian life, is the precise opposite of what we fear. The boundary-less life, the life of the compliant people-pleaser, does not lead to deep and authentic connection. It leads to a profound and painful form of loneliness—the loneliness of being surrounded by people who only know a carefully curated, resentful version of you. It is the loneliness of the performer, who is applauded for their mask but is never truly seen or known.

The courageous, boundary-setting life, on the other hand, is the only path to the authentic relationships our souls truly crave. Healthy boundaries do not destroy relationships; they are the very thing that makes them real. They are not walls that keep people out; they are the fences that protect a sacred space where honesty, trust, and genuine love can finally flourish. This is the final and greatest reward: trading the exhausting performance of obligation for the life-giving joy of authentic connection.

The Death of Resentment, The Birth of Authenticity

At the heart of every boundary-less relationship is a slow-acting poison: resentment. As we have seen, the "resentful yes"—the "yes" you give when your heart is screaming "no"—is a dishonest act. It is a betrayal of your own soul, and it is a subtle deception toward the other person. You are presenting a false self, a persona who is endlessly available, endlessly capable, and endlessly agreeable. The relationship, then, is not with the real you, but with this fictional character you have created. And the real you, the one who is tired, who has limits, who has different priorities, is left feeling invisible, unheard, and profoundly alone.

This is the breeding ground for resentment. Every time you give a resentful "yes," you add another small drop of poison to the well of the relationship. On the surface, you are being "nice," but on the inside, a bitter root is growing. You begin to see the other person not as a friend to be loved, but as a demand to be managed. You start to dread their calls. You see their name in your inbox and your stomach tightens. The relationship, which was meant to be a source of life, becomes a source of draining obligation.

Setting your first, honest boundary is like introducing the antidote to this poison. It is an act of profound authenticity. When you say, "I'm sorry, I can't do that," you are, for perhaps the first time, allowing the real you to show up in the relationship. You are saying, "This is who I am. I have limits. I have priorities. I am not the endlessly capable superhero you thought I was. I am human." This is an act of incredible vulnerability. It is a risk. But it is the only way for a real relationship to begin.

When you are authentic about your limits, you give the other person a precious gift: the opportunity to know and love the real you. Any relationship that cannot survive your authenticity was not a real relationship to begin with; it was a transaction based on your performance. The people who are meant to be in your life, the ones who are capable of genuine love, will respond to your honesty with respect. Your courage will give them permission to be authentic about their own limits, and a new, more honest dynamic can be born. The death of resentment always precedes the birth of authenticity.

The Shift from Obligation to Honor

The Apostle Paul gives us the charter for this new kind of relationship in his letter to the Romans. He writes, "Let love be genuine. Abhor what is evil; hold fast to what is good. Love one another with brotherly affection. Outdo one another in showing honor" (Romans 12:9-10). This short passage is a roadmap for the authentic connections that boundaries make possible.

First, Paul commands, "Let love be genuine." The Greek word for "genuine" here is anypokritos, which literally means "without hypocrisy" or "unmasked." This is the very definition of an authentic, bounded life. The love of a people-pleaser is, by its nature, hypocritical. It wears the mask of service to hide the face of resentment or fear. A bounded life allows you to take off the mask. It allows your love to be sincere because your "yes" is now a free and joyful gift, not a coerced payment to keep the peace. When you have the freedom to say "no," your "yes" becomes an act of genuine, unmasked love.

Second, Paul tells us to "outdo one another in showing honor." This is the beautiful, two-way street of a healthy relationship. To honor someone is to assign them great value, to see them as a person of worth and distinction, made in the image of God. In a boundary-less relationship, this honor is often one-sided. The people-pleaser honors the other person's needs and desires above their own, while their own needs are dishonored and trampled.

When you begin to set healthy boundaries, you are, in effect, teaching people how to honor you. You are demonstrating that you are a person of value, whose time, energy, and calling are worthy of respect. This is not an act of arrogance; it is an act of stewardship. And in doing so, you create a dynamic of mutual honor. A healthy person will see your example of self-respect and learn to honor your limits. And because you are no longer drained by resentment, you are free to more joyfully and authentically honor them. The relationship shifts from a one-way street of demand into a beautiful dance of mutual respect and affection.

The Gift of Safety

One of the most profound and unexpected fruits of a well-bounded life is that you become a "safe" person. This may seem counterintuitive. We think that being endlessly agreeable makes us safe and approachable. But in reality, a person with no boundaries is emotionally unpredictable and, therefore, unsafe. You never know which "yes" will be the one that pushes them over the edge into a passive-aggressive meltdown. You never know if their smile is genuine or if it is masking a deep well of resentment. You are constantly walking on eggshells, trying to guess their true feelings and limits because they will not tell you themselves.

A person with clear, consistent, and graciously communicated boundaries, on the other hand, is a haven of safety. People know where they stand with you. They don't have to guess what you're thinking. They know you will tell them the truth with kindness. They know you won't say "yes" and then make them pay for it with your bad attitude. They know you won't try to rescue them or control them, because you have a clear sense of where your responsibility ends and theirs begins.

This safety creates the space for true intimacy and vulnerability to flourish. When a friend knows that you will listen to their struggles without immediately trying to "fix" them or take on their problems as your own, they feel safe to share their heart. When your adult children know that you will offer your love and support without trying to control their decisions, they feel safe to invite you into their lives. When your spouse knows that you will be honest about your needs and limits, they feel safe to be honest about theirs, and the marriage can grow into a true partnership of mutual care.

This safety is a rare and precious gift in our anxious and chaotic world. To be a safe harbor for the people you love, a non-anxious presence in their lives, is one of the greatest callings of a Christian. And it is a calling that is only possible for the person who is securely anchored by healthy, God-honoring boundaries.

The Joy of a Freely Given "Yes"

This brings us to the ultimate joy of a bounded life. We began this journey by learning to say "no," but we end it by rediscovering the profound and beautiful power of "yes." The "yes" of a boundary-less person is a tired, diluted, and often joyless thing. It is spread so thin across so many obligations that it loses its strength and its savor. But the "yes" of a person who has learned the art of the strategic "no" is a different thing entirely. It is a focused, wholehearted, and joyful gift.

When you have created margin in your life, when you have cleared your plate of the clutter of obligation and fear-based commitments, you are free to give your "yes" with an unreserved and joyful heart. When you say "yes" to helping a friend move, you can do it with a genuine smile, because you are not secretly fuming about the five other things you "should" be doing. When you say "yes" to teaching that Sunday school class, you can pour your heart into the preparation, because you have protected the time and energy to do it well. When you say "yes" to a date night with your spouse, you can be fully present, because you are not mentally running through a list of resentful commitments.

The people in your life no longer get the exhausted, resentful leftovers of your time and energy. They get the best of you. They get your focused attention, your creative energy, and your joyful service. Your acts of love are transformed from draining duties into delightful expressions of a full and grateful heart. This is the abundant life. It is the life where our relationships, once a source of stress and obligation, become a wellspring of mutual joy, genuine fellowship, and life-giving connection.

Conclusion: The Garden Where Love Grows

The fear that boundaries will leave you alone is a lie, whispered by the enemy of our souls who wants to keep us trapped in the lonely prison of performance. The truth of the gospel is that healthy limits are the very thing that sets us free to love and be loved in the way God always intended.

Boundaries are not the cold, stone walls of a fortress designed to keep people out. They are the warm, wooden fences around a garden. They are the structures that protect the tender soil of our hearts from being trampled and compacted by the constant traffic of demands and expectations. Inside this protected space, the seeds of authenticity, trust, and mutual honor can finally take root. And in that well-tended soil, the beautiful, life-giving fruit of genuine, loving relationships can grow, flourish, and ripen in the sun of God's grace.

This is the final harvest. This is the ultimate reward. It is the joy of being fully known and fully loved, and of being free to fully know and fully love others in return. It is the joy of relationships that are no longer a burden to be carried, but a blessing to be cherished. It is the joy of coming home.

Reflection Questions:

1. Think of a relationship in your life that feels more like an obligation than a joy. How has the dynamic of a "resentful yes" contributed to this feeling?

2. Romans 12:9 calls for love to be "genuine" or "unmasked." What is one "mask" you wear in a key relationship? What would it look like to courageously and lovingly take that mask off by setting a boundary?

3. In what ways could you be a "safer" person for the people you love? How might clearer boundaries on your part reduce relational anxiety for

them?

4. Describe the difference in how it feels to give a "yes" out of obligation versus a "yes" that is a free and joyful gift. What is one area where you would like to experience more of that joyful giving?

A Prayer for Authentic Connection

Father, you have created me for connection, for deep and authentic relationships that reflect Your love. Forgive me for the times I have settled for the loneliness of performance instead of pursuing the joy of authenticity. Heal my heart of resentment and replace it with genuine, unmasked love. Give me the courage to be honest about my limits, and the grace to honor the limits of others. Lord, make me a safe person, a haven of stability and peace for those you have placed in my life. Free me to give my "yes" with a whole and joyful heart. May my relationships be transformed from sources of stress into wellsprings of life, for my good and for Your glory. Amen.

Conclusion

The Courage to Say No, The Freedom to Gain Respect

We began this journey together facing a common problem: the tyranny of a life without limits, a life that felt formless and void, governed by the endless demands of others. We have traveled from the very dawn of creation, where we saw God Himself bring order to the cosmos by setting boundaries, to the foot of the cross, where we saw Jesus Christ model a life of perfect, purposeful love—a life that required strategic and courageous "no's." We have journeyed inward, confronting the fear of man and the false guilt that kept us in bondage. And we have looked outward, learning the practical art of speaking the truth in love and standing firm with gentle strength.

The core truth we have uncovered is simple yet revolutionary: a biblical "no" is never just a rejection of something; it is a powerful affirmation of something better. Your "no" is an act of worship, a declaration that pleasing God is your highest priority. It is an act of wise stewardship, a recognition that the time and energy He has given you are precious gifts to be invested, not squandered. And it is a profound act of love—love for yourself as a person worthy of care, and love for others, offering them the gift of your authentic self rather than the shadow of your resentful compliance.

This book is not a final destination, but a trailhead. The principles we have explored are not a formula to be mastered, but a path to be walked, day by day. You will stumble. You will revert to old patterns. You will have moments where fear shouts louder than faith. In those moments, remember the grace of the

Father. His love for you is not dependent on your perfect performance. Simply get back up, dust yourself off, and take the next small, courageous step. Choose one relationship, one conversation, one decision, and practice.

The life that awaits you on this path is one of profound peace, purpose, and connection. It is the life of a person clothed in the quiet strength and dignity that comes from living for an Audience of One. It is a life that, over time, will earn the deepest and most lasting respect from those around you—not because you were always agreeable, but because you were a person of integrity. You will leave a legacy, not of frantic, scattered activity, but of focused, fruitful love. This is the promise. This is the harvest. This is the abundant life that is found when we have the courage to say no, and in doing so, find the freedom to gain true, Christ-honoring respect.

Blessings on your journey!
Rod Lindemann

Epilogue
The Yes That Made A Difference

The man I described in the prologue—the one who wore his endless affirmations like a badge of honor until they became a crushing weight—feels like a distant memory, a cautionary tale from a life I no longer lead. The journey from that season of burnout, the one that led to my early retirement and the writing of this book, has come full circle. The new path I urged you to follow is one I now walk every day.

Today, I am blessed to serve as a part--time pastor in my local congregation. This role is not a lesser calling, but a wiser one, born from hard-won lessons. I have learned to balance life, to cherish the quiet moments of rest as much as the busy hours of ministry. Most importantly, I have learned the profound difference between an obligatory "yes" and my "best yes"—the one that springs not from guilt or expectation, but from a genuine, joyful calling.

The questions that once haunted me in the fog of exhaustion—"Lord, is this what you wanted? A worker so busy for you that he has no time to be with you?"—have been answered. They are answered in the laughter I share with my family, in the peace I find in personal prayer, and in the renewed energy I bring to ministry. The joy that was once choked out has been restored, vibrant and sustainable. I still enjoy serving immensely, but now I am always on the watch for too many yeses, recognizing the early signs of an empty well.

It truly is a joy to use the gifts and talents God has provided in a way that serves Him, our neighbors, my family, and cares for my own soul. This is not a retreat from service, but a re-engagement with it in its purest form. My story is proof that it is possible to escape the cycle of burnout and find a rhythm of grace.

May you find your own best yes. May you serve with gladness and not with a weary heart. And in all things, may you find the freedom and fulfillment that comes from a life surrendered to His perfect will.

To God be the glory.

Rod Lindemann

Small Group Study Guide

A Note for Leaders

Welcome, group leader! This guide is designed to help you facilitate a rich, transformative discussion based on the book How to Say No, and Gain Respect. Your role is not to have all the answers, but to create a safe, supportive space where members can be honest, vulnerable, and encouraging to one another.

Each chapter's guide is divided into three sections:

Reflecting Inwardly: These questions encourage personal introspection and honest self-assessment.

God's Word in Our Hearts: These questions focus on the biblical principles, helping the group dig deeper into the spiritual truths of the chapter.

Walking It Out: These questions are about practical application, moving the discussion from theory to real-life action.

Encourage members to be patient with themselves and each other. This is a journey of unlearning old habits and embracing a new, godly freedom. Begin each session with prayer, asking the Holy Spirit to guide your time together.

Introduction: The Freedom of a Godly "No"
Reflecting Inwardly (Self-Reflection)

1. On a scale of 1-10, how much do you feel your life is your own versus feeling controlled by the obligations and expectations of others?

2. The introduction mentions the "bitter taste of resentment" and the "heavy weight of burnout." Which of these, if any, do you currently identify with most?

3. What is your immediate, gut-level emotional reaction to the idea of saying "no" to someone? (e.g., fear, guilt, relief, anxiety?)

4. Describe a time you said "yes" when you desperately wanted to say "no." What were the consequences for you emotionally, physically, or spiritually?

5. What are some of your own dreams or callings that you feel have been pushed to the side because of your commitments to others?

God's Word in Our Hearts (Impact of Scripture)

1. The introduction contrasts the "tyranny of 'yes'" with the "abundant life that Jesus promised" (John 10:10). What do you believe "abundant life" truly means? How does a constant, joyless sense of service contradict that promise?

2. How has the concept of a "servant's heart" been taught or modeled to you in the past? Has that model sometimes been interpreted as an inability to say "no"?

3. The book's premise is that "the undisciplined, boundary-less life is not the high calling of a Christian." Discuss whether you agree or disagree with this statement and why.

4. Consider the idea of a "holy art of saying 'no.'" How does framing "no" as something holy, rather than selfish, change your perspective?

5. The goal mentioned is to move from being a people-pleaser to a God-pleaser. What do you think is the fundamental difference between the two?

Walking It Out (Practical Next Steps)

1. Before reading this book, what was your primary motivation for saying "yes" to requests? (e.g., desire to help, fear of conflict, seeking approval, genuine passion).

2. Identify one area of your life (work, family, church, friends) where you feel the most over-committed.

3. What is one small, low-risk "no" you could practice saying this week to build your confidence?

4. Share with the group one hope you have for what you will gain by completing this study.

5. This week, start a journal entry titled "My Yeses and Nos." Simply track how many times you say each word and the emotions associated with them, without judgment.

Chapter 1: In the Beginning: Boundaries
Reflecting Inwardly (Self-Reflection)

1. Before this chapter, did you associate boundaries with love or with restriction? How has that perspective been challenged?

2. The chapter implies we are "more comfortable with chaos than with confrontation." How true is this statement in your life?

3. Describe your personal "garden." What are the things (relationships, responsibilities, passions) that God has given you to tend?

4. Where do you feel you have allowed "weeds"—the priorities and problems of others—to choke out what you are called to cultivate?

5. What does the idea of "rest" mean to you? Do you see it as a gift from God to be protected, or as laziness to be overcome?

God's Word in Our Hearts (Impact of Scripture)

1. Read Genesis 1:3-10 together. Discuss the specific acts of separation God performed (light/darkness, water/sky). What does this reveal about His character and His desire for order?

2. Explore the boundary God set in the Garden of Eden (Genesis 2:16-17). How was this boundary an expression of His provision and protection, not just a restriction?

3. The Sabbath was a boundary on time (Exodus 20:8-11). How does honoring the Sabbath—or a principle of intentional rest—protect us from the chaos of endless work?

4. The chapter connects our identity as image-bearers of God to our calling to be cultivators. How does setting boundaries help us better reflect

God's image to the world?

5. Adam was commanded to "work it and keep it" (Genesis 2:15). How does this apply to the non-physical aspects of our lives, like our emotional health, our time, and our spiritual capacity?

Walking It Out (Practical Next Steps)

1. Name one specific "weed" in your life that is draining your energy or time. What is one step you can take to "pull" it this week?

2. Look at your calendar for the coming week. Where can you intentionally build a "fence" of rest, scheduling a time where you are unavailable for a non-emergency request?

3. Practice defining what is "yours to keep." Make a list of your primary responsibilities (e.g., your marriage, your children, your health, your core job functions).

4. Identify a relationship where your boundaries feel blurry or undefined. What is one small way you can bring clarity to that relationship this week?

5. Spend 10 minutes in prayer asking God to show you the "garden" He has entrusted to you. Ask for wisdom to know what to cultivate and what to prune.

Chapter 2: The Law of Love: Boundaries in the Old Testament
Reflecting Inwardly (Self-Reflection)

1. Growing up, did you view the Ten Commandments primarily as a list of "don'ts" or as a guide to freedom?

2. Which of the "horizontal" commandments (5-10) do you find most challenging to navigate in terms of setting personal boundaries? (e.g., honoring parents without being controlled by them, not coveting others' lives).

3. The chapter infers a proverb as "a small fence of wisdom." What is one piece of parental or mentor wisdom that has served as a protective boundary in your life?

4. Consider the "boundary of integrity" (Proverbs 10:9). Can you recall a time when telling a "small lie" to avoid saying "no" created more trouble than it was worth?

5. How do you typically react when your "emotional well" feels dry? Do you withdraw, become irritable, or push through?

God's Word in Our Hearts (Impact of Scripture)

1. Read Exodus 20:1-17 as a group. Discuss how each commandment, when followed by a society, creates a safe and trustworthy community.

2. Focus on the first commandment: "You shall have no other gods before me." How can our desire for approval from others become a form of idol worship?

3. Let's discuss Proverbs 4:23: "Keep your heart with all vigilance, for from it flow the springs of life." What does it practically mean to "guard your heart"? How are boundaries a tool for this?

4. Proverbs 25:28 says a person without self-control is like a "city broken into and left without walls." In what areas of life do you feel "without walls" and vulnerable to attack?

5. How does the concept of God's holiness (His "set-apart-ness") provide a model for our own need for healthy separation and boundaries?

Walking It Out (Practical Next Steps)

1. Identify one "idol" of approval in your life—a person whose opinion you fear or crave too much. What is one step you can take to place God's opinion above theirs?

2. Practice building a "fence of wisdom" this week. Before making a significant commitment, pause and ask yourself: "Is this wise? Does this align with my primary responsibilities?"

3. What is one thing that "refills your well"? Make a non-negotiable appointment with yourself this week to do it.

4. Think of a recurring situation where you lack self-control (e.g., gossiping, overcommitting, mindless scrolling). What is one small, practical "wall" you can build in that area?

5. Choose one proverb mentioned in the chapter. Write it on a notecard and place it somewhere you will see it daily as a reminder.

Chapter 3: The Example of Christ: When Jesus Said No
Reflecting Inwardly (Self-Reflection)

1. Before reading this chapter, did you think of Jesus as someone who ever said "no"? Why or why not?

2. Which example of Jesus's boundaries resonated with you the most: His protection of His time, His identity, or His purpose?

3. Do you ever feel that your schedule is dictated more by the "urgent" demands of others than by your God-given mission?

4. Think about the "temptations" you face that try to pull you away from your core identity in Christ. What are they?

5. How do you feel about the idea of strategic withdrawal or solitude? Does it feel refreshing or selfish to you?

God's Word in Our Hearts (Impact of Scripture)

1. Read Mark 1:35-39. Jesus withdrew to pray even when "everyone" was looking for him. What does this teach us about the importance of communion with the Father over the demands of the crowd?

2. In Matthew 4:1-11, Jesus's response to every temptation was, "It is w ritten..." How does knowing and using Scripture serve as a boundary against the devil's lies about our identity?

3. Consider Jesus's refusal to perform a sign for the Pharisees (Matthew 12:38-39). He said "no" to their demand for a performance. In what ways do we sometimes feel pressured to "perform" for others' approval?

4. Jesus delegated responsibility to His disciples (Luke 10:1-2). How does entrusting others with tasks, rather than doing everything ourselves,

reflect Christ's model of leadership?

5. In the Garden of Gethsemane, Jesus prayed, "not my will, but yours, be done" (Luke 22:42). How did His ultimate submission to God's "yes" empower Him to say "no" to everything else?

Walking It Out (Practical Next Steps)

1. Identify your "morning prayer place." This week, commit to spending at least 15 minutes there before engaging with the world's demands.

2. What is one "loud voice" in your life that is distracting you from your primary mission? What is a practical step you can take to quiet that voice this week?

3. Practice saying, "Let me pray about that before I commit." Use this phrase the next time you are asked for something significant.

4. Who is one person you can delegate a task to this week, empowering them and freeing yourself?

5. Write down what you believe is your core, God-given purpose. Post it where you can see it. Use this statement as a filter for future requests.

Chapter 4: The Fear Factor: Saying No to the Fear of Man
Reflecting Inwardly (Self-Reflection)

1. Be honest: Whose disapproval do you fear the most? Why does that person's opinion hold so much power over you?

2. The chapter calls the fear of man a "snare." Describe a time you felt trapped by your need for someone's approval.

3. What is your typical "conflict style"? Do you avoid it at all costs, accommodate immediately, or face it head-on?

4. In what relationships do you feel like you're wearing a mask, pretending to be someone you're not in order to be accepted?

5. What's the worst-case scenario you imagine happening if you were to say "no" to a key person in your life?

God's Word in Our Hearts (Impact of Scripture)

1. Read Proverbs 29:25 aloud. Discuss the contrast between the "snare" of fearing man and the "safety" of trusting God. What does that safety feel like in a practical sense?

2. Galatians 1:10 is a powerful declaration: "Am I now trying to win the approval of human beings, or of God?" How does this verse challenge the core of people-pleasing?

3. Jesus asked the Pharisees, "How can you believe, when you receive glory from one another and do not seek the glory that comes from the only God?" (John 5:44). How does seeking human praise block our ability to have true faith?

4. Consider the prophet Samuel, who feared the people's reaction but

obeyed God anyway (1 Samuel 16:1-2). Where do we need to choose obedience over popularity?

5. The fear of the Lord is called the "beginning of wisdom" (Proverbs 9:10). How does cultivating a reverent awe of God shrink our fear of human opinion?

Walking It Out (Practical Next Steps)

1. Identify one specific fear that holds you back from setting a boundary (e.g., "They will get angry," "They will think I'm selfish"). Bring that specific fear to God in prayer.

2. Practice an "Audience of One" mindset. Before making a decision this week, consciously ask yourself, "What would please God here?" rather than "What will they think?"

3. Memorize Galatians 1:10. Repeat it to yourself the next time you feel the pull of people-pleasing.

4. Share with the group one small step of courage you can take this week to defy the fear of man in a specific situation.

5. End your day by journaling one way you chose to trust God over fearing a person's reaction, even if it was a small victory.

Chapter 5: The Guilt Complex: Saying No to False Responsibility
Reflecting Inwardly (Self-Reflection)

1. Do you more often feel the "prick" of true conviction from the Holy Spirit or the "heavy blanket" of false guilt? How can you tell the difference?

2. Who in your life is most likely to "guilt-trip" you? What does that typically look like or sound like?

3. Describe a "load" (a personal responsibility) that you are carrying well. Describe a "burden" (someone else's crisis) that you are helping someone with in a healthy way.

4. Are there any "burdens" you have picked up and started carrying as if they were your own permanent "load"?

5. Do you ever feel responsible for other people's happiness or emotional state? How does that affect your decisions?

God's Word in Our Hearts (Impact of Scripture)

1. Read Galatians 6:2-5 carefully. Discuss the difference between a "burden" (baros) and a "load" (phortion). How does understanding this distinction bring freedom?

2. Jesus said, "My yoke is easy, and my burden is light" (Matthew 11:30). How does the feeling of being constantly overwhelmed and crushed suggest we might be carrying a yoke that isn't from Him?

3. 2 Corinthians 9:7 says, "Each one must give as he has decided in his heart, not reluctantly or under compulsion, for God loves a cheerful giver." How does this verse free us from giving motivated by guilt?

4. Consider the story of Mary and Martha (Luke 10:38-42). Martha was "anxious and troubled about many things" she felt responsible for. How did Jesus lovingly correct her sense of false responsibility?

5. The blood of Christ "cleanses our conscience from dead works to serve the living God" (Hebrews 9:14). How can we apply the gospel to our feelings of false guilt?

Walking It Out (Practical Next Steps)

1. Identify one specific "false responsibility" you are carrying. Verbally release it to God in prayer, saying, "God, this is not my load to carry. I trust You with this."

2. The next time you feel a pang of guilt for saying "no," pause and ask: "Is this from the Holy Spirit, or is this from my own fear/someone else's expectation?"

3. Practice the phrase: "I can't carry that for you, but I can walk with you while you carry it." Discuss with the group what this might look like in a real situation.

4. Make a physical list of your God-given "loads" (your spouse, kids, job, etc.). When asked to take on something new, compare it to your list to see if you truly have capacity.

5. If you are struggling with a pattern of manipulation in a relationship, share it with a trusted friend or mentor and ask for prayer and accountability.

Chapter 6: The Stewardship Mandate: Saying Yes to God's Priorities
Reflecting Inwardly (Self-Reflection)

1. If your time and energy were a financial budget, would you say you are "in the black" (have a surplus) or "in the red" (running a deficit)?

2. What are the biggest "time thieves" in your daily life?

3. When you think about your life, what do you want to have "invested" in by the end? What do you want your "return" to be?

4. Does saying "no" feel like a selfish act of deprivation or a wise act of stewardship to you? Why?

5. What is one "good" thing that is currently distracting you from the "best" thing God has for you?

God's Word in Our Hearts (Impact of Scripture)

1. Read the Parable of the Talents in Matthew 25:14-30. What was the master's expectation for his servants? What was the sin of the "wicked, lazy servant"?

2. How does viewing your time, energy, and talents as "talents" (money) entrusted to you by God change the way you think about "spending" them?

3. Ephesians 5:15-16 urges us to "make the best use of the time, because the days are evil." What does it mean to "make the best use of the time" in a practical, daily sense?

4. In the Parable of the Sower (Matthew 13), the seed sown among thorns is "choked by the cares of the world and the deceitfulness of riches." How can over-commitment be one of the "thorns" that chokes out our

spiritual fruitfulness?

5. 1 Corinthians 4:2 states, "it is required of stewards that they be found faithful." How does faithfulness sometimes require us to say "no" to things that would compromise our primary mission?

Walking It Out (Practical Next Steps)

1. Identify your "five-talent" priorities. What are the most important things God has entrusted to you? Write them down.

2. Conduct a "time audit" for one day this week. Track where your hours actually go. Are you surprised by the results?

3. Before you say "yes" to a new commitment, ask this question: "Does this investment align with my God-given priorities and produce the return He is looking for?"

4. Practice saying: "That sounds like a great opportunity, but it falls outside of the main things I'm focused on right now."

5. Identify one "one-talent" activity (a low-yield, time-wasting habit) you can "bury" this week and reinvest that time into a "five-talent" priority.

Chapter 7: Speaking the Truth in Love
Reflecting Inwardly (Self-Reflection)

1. Are you more prone to "brutal, loveless honesty" or "dishonest, truth-less love"? Give an example.

2. What is your biggest fear when it comes to being direct and truthful with someone?

3. Think of a time someone set a boundary with you. What did they do or say that made it feel loving and respectful? What made it feel harsh or rejecting?

4. How does the state of your heart (e.g., angry, resentful, peaceful) affect your tone of voice when you communicate?

5. Do you tend to over-explain or apologize profusely when you say "no"? What do you think is behind that habit?

God's Word in Our Hearts (Impact of Scripture)

1. Read Ephesians 4:15. What is the ultimate goal of "speaking the truth in love"? (To grow up into Christ). How do healthy boundaries contribute to our spiritual maturity?

2. Colossians 4:6 says our speech should be "seasoned with salt." Discuss the three aspects of salt: as a preservative (preserving the relationship), a flavoring (making truth palatable), and a purifier (coming from a pure motive).

3. Jesus said, "out of the abundance of the heart the mouth speaks" (Matthew 12:34). How does this verse convict us to check our motives before we set a boundary?

4. Proverbs 15:1 says, "A soft answer turns away wrath, but a harsh word stirs up anger." How can we apply this to the way we deliver our "no"?

5. In 1 Corinthians 13:4-7, love is described as patient and kind, not arrogant or rude. How can we ensure our boundaries reflect this definition of love?

Walking It Out (Practical Next Steps)

1. Identify a boundary you need to set. First, write down the angry, resentful, unfiltered version. Then, rewrite it using the principles from the chapter (affirming the person, using "I" statements, being clear and kind).

2. Before having a difficult conversation, practice a "heart check." Spend a few minutes in prayer, asking God to purify your motives and fill you with His love for the person.

3. This week, focus on your tone. Practice speaking with a calm, warm, and respectful tone, even when discussing difficult subjects.

4. Choose one person in your life with whom you need to be more truthful. Pray for an opportunity to speak the truth in love to them this week, no matter how small.

5. Practice the "affirming statement" technique. Before you state your "no," start with a sentence that validates the other person or their request (e.g., "Thank you so much for thinking of me," "I really appreciate your passion for this.").

Chapter 8: Scripts for Saying No
Reflecting Inwardly (Self-Reflection)

1. Which scenario in the chapter (family, work, church, friends) feels the most difficult for you to say "no" in? Why?

2. Do you feel you have the "right to pause"? Or do you feel pressured to give an immediate answer to requests?

3. What is your go-to "soft yes" phrase (e.g., "I'll think about it," "Maybe," "We'll see")?

4. Do you believe it's okay to have a different "no" for different relationships, or do you feel you owe everyone the same level of explanation?

5. How do you feel about offering an alternative solution when you say "no"? Does it feel helpful or like you're still taking responsibility?

God's Word in Our Hearts (Impact of Scripture)

1. Read James 1:19: "let every person be quick to hear, slow to speak, slow to anger." How does implementing a strategic pause before answering a request help us live out this verse?

2. Jesus instructed his disciples to be "wise as serpents and innocent as doves" (Matthew 10:16). How does having a prepared, thoughtful "script" for saying "no" reflect this wisdom?

3. Proverbs 18:13 says, "If one gives an answer before he hears, it is his folly and shame." How does pausing and truly listening to a request (even if we know the answer is no) show respect to the other person?

4. In Matthew 5:37, Jesus says, "Let what you say be simply 'Yes' or 'No'; anything more than this comes from evil." How does this challenge our

tendency to over-explain, justify, and equivocate?

5. Galatians 5:1 says, "For freedom Christ has set us free; stand firm there-fore, and do not submit again to a yoke of slavery." How can peo-ple-pleasing be a "yoke of slavery" that we must refuse to submit to?

Walking It Out (Practical Next Steps)

1. Choose one of the scripts from the chapter that you can adapt for your own life. Write it down and practice saying it out loud.

2. This week, your homework is to use the "strategic pause." When some-one asks for something, say: "Let me check my calendar and get back to you by the end of the day."

3. Identify a recurring, draining request in your life. With your small group, brainstorm a loving, firm script to address it.

4. Practice a simple, clear "no" that doesn't over-explain. Try this: "Thank you for the invitation, but I won't be able to make it." Then, stop talking.

5. If appropriate, practice offering a helpful alternative. For example: "I can't commit to volunteering every week, but I would love to help with the one-day event in the fall."

Chapter 9: When Your 'No' Isn't Respected
Reflecting Inwardly (Self-Reflection)

1. Describe a time someone pushed back after you said "no." How did you react? (Did you give in, get angry, defend yourself?)

2. Which pushback tactic are you most vulnerable to: guilt-tripping, questioning your motives, anger, or the "silent treatment"?

3. Do you believe that you are only responsible for your delivery, and the other person is responsible for their reception? Or do you feel responsible for managing their emotions?

4. When someone reacts poorly to your boundary, do you tend to question your decision or stand firm in it?

5. What is the difference between being "Christ-like" (kind but firm) and being a "doormat" (giving in to avoid conflict)?

God's Word in Our Hearts (Impact of Scripture)

1. Read the story of Nehemiah (Nehemiah 6:1-4). Sanballat and Tobiah tried to distract him four times, and each time Nehemiah gave the same clear, firm answer. What can we learn from his persistence?

2. Proverbs 26:4 says, "Answer not a fool according to his folly, lest you be like him yourself." How does this guide us when someone tries to draw us into a manipulative argument over our boundary?

3. Jesus faced constant pushback. In Mark 3:20-22, his own family and the scribes questioned his sanity and motives. How did Jesus respond (or not respond) to these personal attacks?

4. Romans 12:18 says, "If possible, so far as it depends on you, live peace-

ably with all." What does the phrase "so far as it depends on you" mean in the context of setting a necessary boundary?

5. When the rich young ruler walked away sad after Jesus set a hard boundary for him (Matthew 19:21-22), Jesus let him go. What does this teach us about releasing control over other people's choices and reactions?

Walking It Out (Practical Next Steps)

1. Prepare a "broken record" response for a situation where you anticipate pushback. It should be a short, calm, clear sentence you can repeat. (e.g., "I've already made my decision on this," or "I understand you're disappointed, but my answer is still no.")

2. Role-play with someone in your group. Have one person set a boundary and the other person use a pushback tactic. Practice responding calmly and firmly.

3. If you are in a relationship with a highly manipulative or controlling person, what is one step you can take to get support from a pastor, counselor, or trusted mentor?

4. Practice the art of the loving disengagement. If a conversation becomes heated or circular, say: "I'm not willing to argue about this. We can talk later when we're both calm."

5. Write down this sentence and reflect on it: "Their reaction is their responsibility, not mine. My responsibility is to be clear and kind."

Chapter 10: From People-Pleaser to God-Pleaser
Reflecting Inwardly (Self-Reflection)

1. Describe the "chains of expectation" in your life. What unspoken rules do you feel you have to follow to be accepted by a certain person or group?

2. What does the "freedom in Christ" actually feel like to you on a daily basis? Is it a theological concept or a lived reality?

3. Which of the fruits of the Spirit (love, joy, peace, patience, kindness, goodness, faithfulness, gentleness, self-control) do you feel is most lacking in your life due to a lack of boundaries?

4. Describe what it would look like to live for an "Audience of One." What would change about your daily decisions?

5. What old identity (e.g., "the responsible one," "the easy-going one," "the one who always helps") do you need to let go of to embrace your new identity as a God-pleaser?

God's Word in Our Hearts (Impact of Scripture)

1. Read John 8:36: "So if the Son sets you free, you will be free indeed." What are we set free from and what are we set free for?

2. How does cultivating the fruit of "self-control" (Galatians 5:23) directly empower us to set and maintain healthy boundaries?

3. The chapter connects joy and peace with a bounded life. How does a life of constant over-commitment rob us of the joy and peace that are part of our spiritual inheritance?

4. Acts 5:29 gives us the ultimate hierarchy: "We must obey God rather

than men." In what specific area of your life do you need to live out this verse more boldly?

5. Colossians 3:23 says, "Whatever you do, work heartily, as for the Lord and not for men." How can this verse be a guiding principle for the things we say "yes" to and the things we say "no" to?

Walking It Out (Practical Next Steps)

1. Identify one "chain" of human expectation you want to break this week. What is a specific action you can take to do so?

2. Practice "preaching the gospel to yourself." When you feel fear or guilt, remind yourself: "My worth is not in my performance; it is in Christ's finished work on the cross."

3. Choose one fruit of the Spirit you want to cultivate. Ask God how setting a specific boundary might help that fruit to grow in your life.

4. At the end of each day this week, ask yourself one question: "Did I live for God's approval today?" Journal your thoughts.

5. Share with your group one area where you are ready to trade your old identity as a people-pleaser for your true identity as a beloved child of God.

Chapter 11: Earning True Respect
Reflecting Inwardly (Self-Reflection)

1. Do you tend to respect people who have clear boundaries or people who say "yes" to everything? Why?

2. How much self-respect do you currently have? Do you see your own time and energy as valuable resources to be protected?

3. Think of someone you deeply respect. What qualities do they have? How many of those qualities are related to their integrity and clear sense of self?

4. The chapter says an honest "no" is kinder than a resentful "yes." Describe a time you received a "resentful yes" from someone. How did it feel?

5. What is the difference between being "liked" and being "respected"? Which one do you desire more?

God's Word in Our Hearts (Impact of Scripture)

1. Read Titus 2:7-8, which encourages us to show "integrity, dignity, and sound speech that cannot be condemned." How do clear, respectful boundaries contribute to this kind of reputation?

2. Proverbs 22:1 says, "A good name is to be chosen rather than great riches." How can setting boundaries, even when unpopular, actually help build a "good name" for being trustworthy and reliable?

3. Daniel earned the respect of pagan kings (Daniel 6:3) because an "excellent spirit was in him." Part of this was his refusal to compromise his boundaries with God. How does faithfulness to God earn respect from the world?

4. 1 Timothy 4:12 tells Timothy to be an "example... in speech, in conduct, in love, in faith, in purity." How can a young or inexperienced person earn respect by demonstrating these qualities, which are all strengthened by boundaries?

5. How does the Golden Rule, "do to others as you would have them do to you" (Luke 6:31), apply here? If you would want someone to give you an honest "no" rather than a resentful "yes," shouldn't you offer them the same respect?

Walking It Out (Practical Next Steps)

1. What is one action you can take this week to show more respect for your own time and energy? (e.g., scheduling rest, turning off phone notifications).

2. Identify a promise you made with a "resentful yes." Is there a way for you to go back to that person, apologize, and renegotiate the commitment with honesty?

3. Practice this thought pattern: "When I set this boundary, I am teaching people how to treat me with respect."

4. Who is one person you can show respect to this week by being clear and direct with them, rather than vague and non-committal?

5. Journal about the kind of person you want to be. List character qualities. See how many of them are connected to the principles of integrity, honesty, and wise stewardship you've learned in this book.

Chapter 12: Creating Deeper, More Authentic Relationships
Reflecting Inwardly (Self-Reflection)

1. In your closest relationships, do you feel you can be your true self, or do you feel you are playing a role?

2. What does the word "authenticity" mean to you? Do you see it as a positive or a negative trait?

3. How has a lack of boundaries created "superficial harmony" in some of your relationships, hiding unspoken resentment or frustration?

4. Do you consider yourself a "safe" person for others? Can people trust you to be honest and consistent with them?

5. What would it look like for your most important relationships to be built on "mutual honor" instead of "unspoken obligation"?

God's Word in Our Hearts (Impact of Scripture)

1. Read Romans 12:9: "Let love be genuine." The Greek word for "genuine" means "without hypocrisy" or "unmasked." How do boundaries allow us to love others without a mask?

2. Ephesians 4:25 says, "Therefore, having put away falsehood, let each one of you speak the truth with his neighbor, for we are members one of another." How does this verse frame truth-telling as an essential part of being in community?

3. Proverbs 27:6 says, "Faithful are the wounds of a friend; profuse are the kisses of an enemy." How can a loving, boundary-setting "no" be a "faithful wound" that ultimately helps a friend?

4. 1 John 1:7 says that if we "walk in the light, as he is in the light, we have

fellowship with one another." How does hiding our true feelings, needs, and limits keep us from walking in the light and having true fellowship?

5. Jesus called his disciples "friends" (John 15:15) because he was authentic and truthful with them. He shared his heart and his mission. How can we follow His example to build deeper friendships?

Walking It Out (Practical Next Steps)

1. Choose one important relationship where you want to cultivate more authenticity. What is one small step you can take to be more honest about your feelings or limits this week?

2. Practice active listening. The next time a loved one is talking, focus completely on understanding them, rather than on formulating your "yes" or "no."

3. Initiate a "relationship check-in" with your spouse or a close friend. Ask questions like, "Is there any unspoken frustration between us? How can I love you better?"

4. Make a list of the unspoken "rules" in one of your relationships. Are they healthy? Do they need to be discussed openly and lovingly?

5. Celebrate progress. Share with the group one way that setting a boundary has, surprisingly, brought you closer to someone and made the relationship more honest and respectful.

Conclusion: The Courage to Say No, The Freedom to Gain Respect
Reflecting Inwardly (Self-Reflection)

1. Looking back to the start of this study, what has been the biggest change in your perspective on saying "no"?

2. What was the most challenging chapter or concept for you in this book? Why?

3. What was the most freeing or "aha!" moment you experienced during this study?

4. How has your definition of a "good Christian" evolved? What fears still linger as you consider living a more bounded life?

God's Word in Our Hearts (Impact of Scripture)

1. Read Joshua 1:9: "Have I not commanded you? Be strong and courageous. Do not be frightened, and do not be dismayed, for the LORD your God is with you wherever you go." How is this a perfect final command for our journey?

2. This journey has been about moving from a life of slavery to expectations to a life of freedom in Christ (Galatians 5:1). What does that freedom look like for you in the coming weeks and months?

3. Think about the Great Commandment: to love God and love your neighbor (Matthew 22:37-39). How has this study shown you that proper boundaries are essential to fulfilling both parts of this command?

4. Consider 2 Timothy 1:7: "for God gave us a spirit not of fear but of power and love and self-control." Discuss how each of those three gifts—power, love, and self-control—is essential for setting healthy boundaries.

5. How will you continue to steep your heart in God's Word to find the courage and wisdom you need to continue this journey?

Walking It Out (Practical Next Steps)

1. Share with the group the single most important lesson you will take away from this book.

2. What is the one boundary you are most committed to maintaining for the long term?

3. How can this group continue to support and provide accountability for one another as you walk out these principles?

4. Write a letter to your future self, reminding yourself of the freedom and respect you've gained and encouraging yourself not to slip back into old people-pleasing habits.

5. End your time together by praying for one another, asking God for the continued courage to say "no" and the grace to live in the freedom He has so richly provided.

About the Author

Rodney A. Lindemann has built a life centered on faith, family, and service. He has been married to his beloved wife, Miriam, for over 25 years. Together, they have a blended family of four stepchildren, who are all now grown and married, and they are blessed with 14 grandchildren.

A lifelong member of Timothy Lutheran Church, Rod's commitment to his faith led him to be ordained into the office of Public Ministry in 2011. After faithfully serving as an associate pastor, he has since retired into a part-time pastoral role, continuing his passion for ministry. Alongside his spiritual calling, Rod is an entrepreneur and the owner of Rods Sports and Apparel.

Rod's inspiration to write How to Say No and Gain Respect came directly from his own trials and tribulations of saying "yes" too often. Through his experiences, he discovered the importance of setting boundaries to achieve the right balance of priorities: God, family, others, and self. In his free time, Rod enjoys riding motorcycles and cherishing moments with his ever-growing family.

www.ingramcontent.com/pod-product-compliance
Lightning Source LLC
Chambersburg PA
CBHW070338130626
46556CB00007B/2922